SLAVISTIC PRINTINGS
AND REPRINTINGS

SLAVIC FORUM

ESSAYS IN LINGUISTICS
AND LITERATURE

edited by

MICHAEL S. FLIER

1974

MOUTON

THE HAGUE · PARIS

© Copyright 1974 in the Netherlands.
Mouton & Co. N. V., Publishers, The Hague

No part of this book may be translated or reproduced in any form, by print, photoprint, microfilm, or any other means, without written permission from the publishers

491.7008
S631
1974

LIBRARY OF CONGRESS CATALOG CARD NUMBER: 72-88178

Printed in Hungary

TO MY FATHER AND MOTHER

PREFACE

In 1970 the third annual West Coast Summer Program in Slavic and East European Studies was held at UCLA under the auspices of the Department of Slavic Languages, the UCLA Office of Summer Sessions, and the United States Office of Education (under grant no. OEC 0–70–2603). In addition to intensive language courses in Russian, Czech, Serbocroatian, Bulgarian, Estonian, Hungarian, and Romanian, the Summer Program offered numerous area courses in Slavic linguistics, Russian literature and history taught by a distinguished faculty from across the nation, e.g. Alexander V. Isačenko (UCLA): "Russian Lexicology", "Seminar in Aspect and Tense in Russian"; Hans Rogger (UCLA): "Russian Intellectual History", "History of Russia 1796–1917"; George Y. Shevelov (Columbia University): "Introduction to the History and Structure of Ukrainian and Belorussian", "Selected Problems in Comparative Slavic Linguistics"; Kiril Taranovsky (Harvard University): "Russian Poetics", "Seminar in Russian Metrics and Versification"; Robert H. Whitman (University of California, Berkeley): "Generative Russian Syntax"; Dean S. Worth (UCLA): "Russian Derivational Morphology"; Gerta H. Worth (UCLA): "Introduction to the History of the Russian Literary Language". The complete list of staff and curriculum is given below.

During the eight-week session distinguished scholars in the field of Slavic languages and literatures were invited to offer formal presentations weekly in the Slavic Forum Lecture Series on current problems in their own research. With two exceptions[1] the essays in this volume represent the written versions of those presentations except for changes introduced by the authors as a result of the

---

[1] Professors Isačenko and Shevelov delivered lectures which were committed for publication elsewhere.

discussions following each lecture. For thematic continuity the linguistic and literary studies have been grouped together.

As Director of the Summer Program I wish to express my gratitude to the Forum Lecture participants, the faculty, and the administrative staff for making the summer a profitable and rewarding one for all.

MICHAEL S. FLIER
Los Angeles
November, 1970

TABLE OF CONTENTS

Preface 7
1970 West Coast Summer Program in Slavic and East European Studies 11
Slavic Forum Lecture Series—1970 12
A note on transliteration 13

PART ONE: LINGUISTICS

Morris Halle
    Remarks on Slavic accentology 17
Alexander V. Isačenko
    On *have* and *be* languages: A typological sketch 43
Theodore M. Lightner
    A problem in the analysis of some *vowel* ∼ *zero* alternations in Modern Russian 78

PART TWO: LITERATURE

Victor Erlich
    The writer as witness: The achievement of Alexander Solzhenitsyn 91
Donald Fanger
    The Gogol problem: Perspectives from absence 103
Hugh McLean
    Cathedral Folk: Apotheosis of Orthodoxy or its Doomsday Book? 130
Kiril Taranovsky
    The problem of context and subtext in the poetry of Osip Mandel'štam 149

1970 WEST COAST SUMMER PROGRAM IN SLAVIC AND EAST EUROPEAN STUDIES

Elementary Russian	P. Hodgson (UCLA)
Intermediate Russian	P. Hodgson (UCLA)
Advanced Russian	G. Worth (UCLA), M. Gisetti (UCLA)
Russian Composition	D. Worth (UCLA), N. Pavlova (USC)
Elementary Czech	Z. Meyerstein (UCLA)
Elementary Bulgarian	I. Talev (UCLA)
Elementary Serbocroatian	A. Albin (UCLA)
Elementary Estonian	E. Vihman (Berkeley)
Elementary Hungarian	K. Keresztes (American University)
Elementary Romanian	D. Grigorescu (University of Bucharest)
Russian Intellectual History	H. Rogger (UCLA)
Russian History 1796–1917	H. Rogger (UCLA)
Structure of Macedonian	A. Albin (UCLA)
Russian Literature: Nineteenth Century	M. Curran (University of Illinois)
Tolstoy	M. Curran (University of Illinois)
Introduction to the History of the Russian Literary Language	G. Worth (UCLA)
Russian Derivational Morphology .	D. Worth (UCLA)
Generative Russian Syntax	R. Whitman (Berkeley)
Russian Lexicology	A. Isačenko (UCLA)
Russian Poetics	K. Taranovsky (Harvard University)
Introduction to the Structure and History of Ukrainian and Belorussian	G. Shevelov (Columbia University)
Selected Problems in Comparative Slavic Linguistics	G. Shevelov (Columbia University)
Intensive Old Church Slavic	M. Flier (UCLA)
Seminar in Aspect and Tense in Russian	A. Isačenko (UCLA)
Seminar in Russian Metrics and Versification	K. Taranovsky (Harvard University)

ADMINISTRATIVE STAFF

Administrative Assistants for the
  Department of Slavic Languages,
  UCLA .... Mary Pottala, Judy Shulman
Administrative Assistant for the Russian and East European Studies
  Center, UCLA .... Lucille Liets

SLAVIC FORUM LECTURE SERIES — 1970

UNIVERSITY OF CALIFORNIA, LOS ANGELES

23 July   *Alexander V. Isačenko* (UCLA)
"The jer shift in East Slavic: A new morphophonemic approach"

30 July   *Theodore M. Lightner* (University of Texas)
"A synchronic treatment of *jers* in modern Russian"

6 August   *Donald Fanger* (Harvard University)
"The Gogol problem: Perspectives from absence"

13 August   *George Y. Shevelov* (Columbia University)
"The phonological development of Common Slavic from a typological point of view"

20 August   *Hugh McLean* (University of California, Berkeley)
"*Soborjane*: Apotheosis of Orthodoxy or its Doomsday Book?"

27 August   *Morris Halle* (Massachusetts Institute of Technology)
"Remarks on Slavic accentology"

3 September   *Victor Erlich* (Yale University)
"The writer as witness: The achievement of Alexander Solzhenitsyn"

8 September   *Kiril Taranovsky* (Harvard University)
"The problem of context and subtext in the poetry of Osip Mandel'štam"

A NOTE ON TRANSLITERATION

With the exception of certain proper names I have adhered to the international (continental) system of transliterating Cyrillic into Latin letters, e.g. ч = č, ш = š, ц = c, ь = ', ъ = ". I have used traditional English spellings of names which have achieved wide circulation: Chekhov instead of Čexov, Pushkin instead of Puškin, Solzhenitsyn instead of Solženicyn, but Mandel'štam, Vjazemskij, Axmatova.

M. S. F.

PART ONE

LINGUISTICS

REMARKS ON SLAVIC ACCENTOLOGY*

MORRIS HALLE

0. This study of Slavic accentuation has been guided by two considerations that might be termed theoretical in the sense that they do not derive directly from the facts, but are rather ideas concerning the nature and organization of the data arrived at independently of the particular facts to be considered here. The strong empiricist strain dominant in much of modern linguistics has taught us to be rather skeptical about the value of such theoretical considerations. It is widely felt that theory should be closely linked to the facts, and any departure from "a close hugging of the phonetic ground" is regarded by many linguists as the surest road to disaster. This view seems to me quite mistaken. Theory must be more than a more or less elegant summary of the facts known to the theorist. It is only when theory makes claims about facts which are unfamiliar or totally unknown that theory exercises its true function in science, which is that of a tool for the discovery of facts. To illustrate this function of a theory is one of the aims of this paper. Its success or failure, therefore, is to be judged by the extent to which it succeeds or fails to deepen our understanding of the accentology of Slavic languages, which because of its complexity and intricacy has occupied the attention of linguists for a century or more.

The first of the theoretical considerations that play an important role in the present investigation was proposed by Nancy Woo in her dissertation (1969). She argued that "dynamic" tones such as "rising", "falling", or "fall-rise" were not to be included in the universal set of distinctive features; instead whenever phoneticians observed in a language such "dynamic" tones, these had to be

* This work was supported in part by National Institute of Mental Health grant MH – 13390 – 04. In preparing this paper I have received help from Wayles Brown and Horace Lunt, for which I am most grateful. This article is reprinted from *Linguistic Inquiry* 2, 1 (1971) by permission of the MIT Press.

explained as surface manifestations of underlying representations in which only "stationary" tones figure. Thus, for instance, Woo showed that in Northern Tepehuan "falling" and "rising" tones are always surface manifestations of sequences of two vowels, one having a "high" tone and the second, the neutral "nonhigh" tone. When the "high" toned vowel is first in the sequence, we observe "falling" tone; when it is second, we observe "rising" tone. It is, of course, always possible to represent "falling" and "rising" tones in this fashion. The fact that makes Woo's suggestion interesting is that when the "dynamic" tones are so represented the phonological description of Northern Tepehuan is significantly improved. Woo has shown that a similar situation prevails in a number of widely divergent languages, that when "dynamic" tones are treated as purely surface phenomena, not only is there no loss of generalization in the phonological description of the language; instead the description can be deepened. These results are obviously of the greatest interest but they fall short of conclusively establishing Woo's hypothesis concerning the nature of prosodic features, so that further empirical testing of the hypothesis is clearly indicated. The prosodic phenomena of the Slavic languages constitute a good testing ground for Woo's hypothesis, and as will be shown below, provide independent support for the hypothesis in a manner quite different from that of the languages discussed by Woo.

The second theoretical idea that has guided this work was originally advanced by Roman Jakobson in his report to the International Congress of Slavists held at Sofia (1963), and in his contribution to the volume of studies in honor of J. Kurylowicz (1965). In its grossest terms the idea is that underlying all Slavic prosodic phenomena is a pitch contour of the word that is much like that of a "terrace tone" language such as Japanese. In Japanese the word is divided into two parts, an initial high pitched portion, and a final low (or neutral) pitched portion (the latter may be lacking). In order to specify the pitch contour of a word, it is, therefore, necessary only to indicate the vowel after which the low pitched portion of the word begins. This initial marking of the Japanese word is provided by the morphological component of the grammar, for it depends on the morphemic composition of the word. The prosodic contour of the word is established by special phonological rules which characteristically differ from dialect to dialect but always take as their input the word with the specially marked vowel as provided by the morphology. The phonological rules thus complete the specification of the pitch contour of the word. What is especially important here is that the phonetic output is the product of two distinct components, the morphological rules that determine the initial marking of the word, and the phonological rules that derive the phonetic output from forms first operated on by the morphological component. I shall try to show in the discussion that follows that an analogous situation prevails in Slavic; i.e. the prosodic contour of words is determined by the interaction of the two independent components, the morphology and phonology of the particular language. I believe that much of the confusion that permeates Slavic accentological studies is due to a failure to see that two totally distinct components — and hence distinct types of process — are involved.

1. We begin by considering what is perhaps the simplest case, the stress system of modern Russian. We examine the stress contour of the inf. and 2nd sg. present forms

$$v,irt,et, \qquad v,ert,iš \qquad \text{'turn'}$$

where the stressed vowels are represented in bold face. We shall assume that underlying these forms we have the strings

$$v,ert,+e+t, \qquad v,ert,+e+i+š$$

We postulate, moreover, the following rules:

(1) H ASSIGNMENT, which places a diacritic feature [+H] on some vowel in the word. (Note that there are words that do not receive [+H] on any vowel.) This rule is part of the morphology.
H DISTRIBUTION, which places the diacritic feature [+H] on all vowels preceding (to the left of) the vowel marked [+H] by the H ASSIGNMENT rule.
VOWEL TRUNCATION, which deletes a vowel followed by a vowel (cf. Jakobson 1948).
STRESS ASSIGNMENT, which places stress on the last (rightmost) vowel marked [+H]; or, if there is no such vowel, on the first vowel in the word.
NEUTRALIZATION rules, which assign [−H] to all unstressed

vowels, and convert unstressed [o, a, e] → [i] after "soft" consonants *(ikanje)*, and → [ə] elsewhere *(akanje)*.

Given these five rules we derive the correct stress contours from underlying representations as shown:

$v,ert,+e+t,$	$v,ert,+e+i+š$	
+H	+H	H ASSIGNMENT
+H	+H	H DISTRIBUTION
	∅	VOWEL TRUNCATION
e	e	STRESS ASSIGNMENT
i		NEUTRALIZATION
$v,irt,et,$	$v,ert,iš$	

What is important about these derivations is that they capture quite naturally the feature that is at the heart of many Slavic accentual phenomena, i.e. when a potentially stressed vowel is deleted the stress moves towards the front of the word. It is essential to observe that there is no logical reason that this should be the case. It is equally plausible to suppose that when a potentially stressed vowel is deleted the stress moves towards the end of the word, or that the word becomes stressless. It is, therefore, a significant, though perhaps small point in favor of the proposed system of rules that of the three possible alternatives just discussed the rules pick the one that is empirically correct.

The same movement of stress towards the beginning of the word can be observed in forms with a zero desinence. In treating such forms I assume (following Lightner) that in underlying representations of modern Russian there are two reduced vowels, ъ, ь (the so-called *jers*)[1] which either appear on the surface as [o, e] respectively, or are deleted. To account for these facts we shall postulate the two rules:

JER DELETION, which deletes jers word-finally, or if followed by a full vowel in the next syllable.

JER LOWERING, which turns all jers remaining after JER DELETION has applied into [o, e].

---

[1] We leave here unresolved the question as to the phonetic nature of the sounds represented by the symbols ъ, ь.

We shall assume that JER DELETION and JER LOWERING apply after the VOWEL DELETION rule but before the STRESS ASSIGNMENT and NEUTRALIZATION rules. Given these rules we can now show the way in which they operate in the derivation of the stress contours of such words as:

(2)   *stol*   *stala*   'table'   (nom. sg. + gen. sg.)
        zajom   *zajma*   'loan'   (nom. sg. + gen. sg.)
        kiška   *kišok*   'intestine'   (nom. sg. + gen. pl.)

stol+ъ	*stol+a*	*zajьm+ъ*	*zajьm+a*	*kišьk+a*	*kišьk+ъ*	
+H	+H	+H	+H	+H	+H	H ASSIGNMENT
+H	+H	+H	+H	+H+H	+H+H	H DISTRIBUTION
		not applicable				VOWEL TRUNCATION
∅		∅	∅	∅	∅	JER DELETION
		o			o	JER LOWERING
o	a	o	a	a	o	STRESS PLACEMENT
−H	−H		−H		−H	NEUTRALIZATION
stol	*stala*	*zajom*	*zajma*	*kiška*	*kišok*	

As noted above the actual placement of stress is determined by two separate factors: on the one hand, there are the phonological rules and, on the other hand, there are special morphological or readjustment rules — here represented by the H ASSIGNMENT rule — which assign the feature [+H] in the first place. In a way this division into two components is implicit in the traditional historical treatment of the problem, except that instead of assigning the feature [+H] which we shall identify as the equivalent of the phonetic feature HIGH PITCH, the traditional historical treatment postulated that special intonations were assigned by these rules: when the stress was on the stem as in the case of *zajom*, it was said that the stem had ACUTE intonation; when it was on the desinence as in the word *kiška*, it was said to be OXYTONE, and when the word would have remained without [+H] by our rules, the traditional description said that it had CIRCUMFLEX intonation on the first syllable.[2] Sound laws (among them the much debated Law of Saussure-Fortunatov) as well as analogy were then adduced to account for the present day state of affairs in the individual languages.

In contrast to the traditional view I would regard the various classes of stems as being distinguished from one another not by means of a phonetic mark, but rather by means of a special morpho-

---

[2] We shall have something to say about the fourth class of words, the so-called neoacute, in the discussion below.

logical classifier, similar perhaps to the marker that tells us that in Latin *campus* belongs to the fourth declension, whereas *amicus* belongs to the second declension. I take it that such markers are utilized by the H ASSIGNMENT rule to determine which vowel (if any) is to be marked [+H]. In a study of the accentual pattern of the Russian nominal declension (Halle 1970) I suggested that Russian noun stems basically are categorized into four classes depending on whether or not they require desinential stress in the singular, the plural, in neither number, or in both numbers. In addition, there is a small number of nouns that require further subcategorization. Whether this type of classification can be shown to hold for the accentual patterns observed in other types of words as well, is at present an open question which in my opinion is both of utmost difficulty and importance. I hope to devote to it a major investigation in the not too distant future.[3]

2. The set of rules that has been developed above can handle the prosodic contours of words in Slavic languages other than Russian with only minor modifications. Consider first Standard Serbo-Croatian, Štokavian. As is well known this dialect has four types of accented vowel: short rising ´, long rising ˋ, short falling ˮ, long falling ˆ. The rising and falling tones do not occur freely in all positions in the word, as shown in Table 1 below (adapted from Ivič 1958):

TABLE 1

	Monosyllabic words	Polysyllabic words		
		Initially	Finally	Medially
Falling	Yes	Yes	No	No
Rising	No	Yes	No	Yes

[3] While this paper was in press I have had the opportunity to read the interesting dissertation of Herbert S. Coats (1970), which has shown me that the scheme proposed in Halle (1970) is in need of some revision. In particular Coats' study has made clear for me the absolutely pivotal position that is occupied in Russian phonology by a METATONY rule very similar to the identically named rule (22) of Slovenian discussed below. It is this rule rather than the H ASSIGNMENT which is responsible for the stem stress in plural forms of nouns with desinential stress in the sg. such as *čislo* 'number', *vereteno* 'spindle', *beda* 'sorrow', *sirota* 'orphan'. This result must be incorporated into any future study.

These facts can be readily accounted for if we make two assumptions. First, we assume that Standard Štokavian had a system of stress rules much like Russian, except that the STRESS ASSIGNMENT rule locates the stress not on the last vowel with [+H], but rather on the penultimate vowel with [+H], if possible. In cases where only the first vowel in the word has [+H], this vowel receives the stress; and when no vowel has [+H] the first syllable in the word (including here the preposition, if any) is stressed. Second, we propose that the term "rising tone" in the traditional literature refers to a stressed vowel which is FOLLOWED IN THE SAME WORD BY A VOWEL WITH [+H], whereas all other stressed vowels are said to have "falling" tone. Phonetically this makes good sense for we have assumed that [+H] represents the tonal feature [High pitch], and, in fact, Ivić and Lehiste have shown in their detailed acoustic investigations of Standard Štokavian tones (1963) that "while the distinction between the two long accents might conceivably be based on information in the accented syllables themselves, in the case of the two short accents this information is decidedly insufficient. The feature which was constantly present and appeared to carry the main burden of distinction was the relationship between the stressed and the post-tonic syllable. In the case of both the short and the long falling accents, the post-tonic syllable had a low fundamental frequency (or there was no post-tonic syllable in the same word — M. H.); in the case of both rising accents, the post-tonic syllable had a fundamental frequency that was either the same or higher than that of the preceding syllable" (p. 132).

Returning now to the facts represented in Table 1 we see that these are readily accounted for in terms of the Standard Štokavian stress rule and the interpretative convention proposed above. Since "rising" tone is the tone of a stressed vowel followed in the same word by a vowel with [+H], it follows immediately that "rising" tone cannot be found on the last syllable of polysyllabic words or on monosyllabic words, but can, of course, be found elsewhere. Since the stress in polysyllabic words is placed on the penultimate vowel with [+H], if possible, we shall have "rising" tone in polysyllabic words in all cases except when the H ASSIGNMENT rule either marks only the first vowel in the word or leaves the word unmarked. In this case, stress will be assigned to the first syllable of the word and the stressed vowel will have "falling" tone since it is NOT followed by a vowel with [+H]. Thus "falling" tone can be found only on the first or only syllable of the word as indicated in Table 1.

The facts represented in Table 1 are quite complex. They are handled with great simplicity and naturalness by the rule system proposed above. As this could hardly be an accidental byproduct of our rule system we take the case just examined as further evidence supporting the approach that we have taken here.

In addition to accounting for the peculiar distributions of the tones as well as being supported by the surface phonetics, the proposed stress assignment rule and the convention on interpreting "rising" and "falling" tones explains also the fact well known to all students of comparative Slavic accentology that in cognate words the accented vowel with "falling" tone in Standard Štokavian corresponds to the stressed vowel in Russian, whereas the accented vowel with "rising" tone in Standard Štokavian corresponds to the pretonic vowel in Russian.

(3)   Štokavian "falling" tones
      vȍdu 'water'   nȍsiš 'carry'   lȉpa 'linden'   zûba 'tooth'
      (acc. sg.)   (2nd sg.)   (gen. sg.)

      Russian
      v**o**du 'water'   n**o**s,iš 'carry'   l,**i**pa 'linden'   z**u**ba 'tooth'
      (acc. sg.)   (2nd sg.)   (gen. sg.)

      Štokavian "rising" tones
      sèstra 'sister'   jèzik 'tongue'   národa 'people'
                                          (gen. sg.)

      Russian
      s,ist**ra** 'sister'   jiz**y**k 'tongue'   nar**o**da 'people'
                                          (gen. sg.)

Needless to say, there are substantial differences between the Russian and Štokavian rules for [+H] assignment, but to the extent that these are the same, the difference in surface phonetics reflects differences between the Russian and Štokavian STRESS ASSIGNMENT and NEUTRALIZATION rules, of which, for our purposes, the former is the more important one.

3. We next turn to a different dialect of Serbo-Croatian, the Čakavian dialect of Noví which, for good reason, has occupied a central portion in all discussions of Slavic accentology ever since it was described by Belić in 1909. This dialect has, like those already exam-

ined, a rule assigning [+H] which, except for certain deviations of detail, corresponds to that of Russian and Štokavian. It also has an H DISTRIBUTION rule and a STRESS ASSIGNMENT rule. The last of these is exactly like that of Russian, not of Štokavian, in that it assigns stress to the last [+H] in the word.

(4)   Noví   Russian

     gorȁ   gará   'mountain'   (nom. sg.)
     gȍru   góru   (acc. sg.)
     gȍre   góry   (nom. pl.)
     gorȁmi   garámi   (instr. pl.)

If we assume that "rising" tone is, as in Štokavian, the consequence of a stressed vowel followed by a vowel with high pitch, then clearly we cannot expect this dialect to have vowels with "rising" tone. The dialect, however, has "rising" tones. According to all investigators, these "rising" tones are not identical with the rising tones of Štokavian. One's first impulse would be to say that the "rising" tone in the Noví dialect is to be represented by the feature [+Rise].[4] This move, however, is one that I should like to avoid, for, as noted above, Nancy Woo has given strong reasons for believing that the framework of prosodic features does not include such dynamic tones as "rise" or "fall". As it is impossible at this point to resolve this question we shall provisionally introduce the feature [+R] to designate the "rising" tone of Noví. I return to this question in the discussion of the Slovene data below, where a new interpretation is offered that leaves Nancy Woo's proposed limitation intact.

We assume, therefore, provisionally that in the Noví dialect there is operative a rule — we shall call it the NEOACUTE rule — which assigns the feature [+R] to stressed vowels. Our task now is to characterize the conditions under which the NEOACUTE rule applies. The conditions show up most clearly in the examples (5) which should be compared with the Russian verbs discussed in §1.

(5)   žènit 'marry' (inf.)   žěniš (2nd sg.)
     pãlit 'burn' (inf.)   pãliš (2nd sg.)

---

[4] We distinguish the Štokavian rising tone from the Čakavian and Slovene by using the diacritics ′ ` for the former and the diacritic ~ for the latter. We use " ⁀ to represent the falling short and long tones respectively in all South Slavic languages.

If we assume underlying representations like those postulated for the Russian verbs in é 1, we get

$$\begin{array}{cccc} \check{z}en+i+t & \check{z}en+i+\bar{\imath}+\check{s} & p\bar{a}l+i+t & p\bar{a}l+i+i\check{s} \\ +\text{H} & +\text{H} & +\text{H} & +\text{H} \quad \text{H ASSIGNMENT} \end{array}$$

We observe immediately that the neoacute appears on a long vowel which in the underlying representation precedes a vowel with [+H]. However, as the infinitive form $p\bar{a}l\tilde{\imath}t$ shows, not every long vowel in this position has rising stress but only the long vowel that ends up with the stress. To achieve the result we need, we have to assume that the Noví dialect differs from the dialects reviewed so far in that before the TRUNCATION rule it incorporates a NEOACUTE rule which assigns the feature [+R] to a long vowel when followed by a vowel with [+H]. In addition the dialect is subject to a NEUTRALIZATION rule which applies after the STRESS ASSIGNMENT rule and makes all unstressed vowels $\begin{bmatrix} -\text{R} \\ -\text{H} \end{bmatrix}$. With these modifications we can derive the correct stress contours as shown:

$\check{z}en+i+t$	$\check{z}en+i+\bar{\imath}+\check{s}$	$p\bar{a}l+i+t$	$p\bar{a}l+i+\bar{\imath}+\check{s}$	
+H	+H	+H	+H	H ASSIGNMENT
+H	+H	+H	+H	H DISTRIBUTION
—	—	+R	+R	NEOACUTE
—	∅	—	∅	TRUNCATION
—	—	—	—	JER DELETION
—	—	—	—	JER LOWERING
i	e	i	$\bar{a}$	STRESS ASSIGNMENT
$\begin{bmatrix}-\text{H}\\-\text{R}\end{bmatrix}$	—	$\begin{bmatrix}-\text{H}\\-\text{R}\end{bmatrix}$	—	NEUTRALIZATION
$\check{z}en\check{\imath}t$	$\check{z}\check{e}n\bar{\imath}\check{s}$	$p\bar{a}l\check{\imath}t$	$p\bar{a}l\bar{\imath}\check{s}$	OUTPUT

We can immediately test our proposal because we know of another set of forms where the neoacute ought to appear, i.e. in forms where a weak jer must be assumed to have [+H], e.g. in oxytone nouns similar to the Russian *stol – stalá*. And indeed we find as shown in (6a) that when such nouns have a long stem vowel they manifest rising tone; when the stem vowel is short, the tone is falling as shown in (6b).

(6) a. $b\tilde{a}n - b\bar{a}n\grave{\imath}$ 'governor' $br\tilde{e}st - br\bar{e}st\grave{a}$ 'elm' $s\tilde{u}d - s\bar{u}d\grave{a}$ 'law court'
$l\tilde{\imath}h - l\bar{\imath}h\grave{a}$ 'garden' $gl\tilde{a}v - gl\bar{a}v\grave{a}$ 'head' $tr\tilde{a}v - tr\bar{a}v\grave{a}$ 'grass'

b. *krȍv – krovà̀* 'roof'   *bȍb – bobà̀* 'pea'   *bȁt – batà̀* 'club'
mȁst – mastà̀ 'juice'   *čȅp – čepà̀* 'stopper'   *pȍp – popà̀* 'priest'

The examples in (6a) and (5) are not the only cases where we find "rising" tone in the Noví dialect. It appears, for instance, in such forms as those in (7) which differ thus strikingly from those in (6b):

(7)   *stõl – stolà̀* 'table'   *dvõr – dvorà̀* 'yard'   *sestãr – sestrà̀* 'sister'
stãrca – stãrac 'old man'

The simplest way to handle these cases would be by postulating a special rule that assigns both length and "rising" tone — i.e. $\begin{bmatrix} +\text{R} \\ +\text{long} \end{bmatrix}$ — to stressed vowels before a liquid which may be word final or followed by at least one consonant; i.e. in the environment [X___L(C$_1$Y)]. The proposed rule would have to apply after stress assignment and clearly cannot be combined in any way with the NEOACUTE rule.

A case of considerably greater interest is provided by the existence in the Noví dialect of such accentual doublets of the loc. pl. forms as those in (8):

(8) a.   *vlāsīh* 'hair'   *brēstīh* 'elm'   *krovīh* 'roof'
  b.   *vlāsīh*   *brēstīh*   *krȍvīh*

We can readily obtain the forms in (8a) by assuming the H ASSIGNMENT rule assigns [+H] to the word final jer of the inflectional ending. The output is then derived in the manner of (9):

(9)   *krovīhъ*
    +H   H ASSIGNMENT
  +H+H   H DISTRIBUTION
    +R   NEOACUTE
    — —   VOWEL TRUNCATION
    ∅   JER DELETION
    — —   JER LOWERING
    ī   STRESS ASSIGNMENT
    —H   NEUTRALIZATION
   krovīh   OUTPUT

On the other hand to obtain *krȍvīh* and the rest of the examples in (8b) we must assume that the dialect is subject to a special RETRAC-

TION rule (10) which if it is made to apply before JER DELETION and before STRESS ASSIGNMENT can be stated as in (10).

(10)　RETRACTION

$$V \rightarrow \begin{bmatrix} -H \\ -R \end{bmatrix} \bigg/ \begin{bmatrix} X \underline{\quad} C_0 \begin{Bmatrix} ъ \\ ь \end{Bmatrix} \end{bmatrix} \text{ in certain cases}$$

It can readily be seen that this would give the correct outputs for the forms in (8b). It must also be noted that the RETRACTION rule is what has been called a "minor" rule, i.e. a rule whose application is highly restricted both morphologically and lexically. Belic (1909) suggests that "if the medial (i.e. stem — M. H.) syllable is short the stress goes to the very end, whereas if it is long the stress (and it is ˜) is on that syllable". (p. 210) Hence we get

(11) a. so*kolĩh* 'falcon'　*prstenĩh* 'ring' (with short stem vowels)

　　 b. *golũbĩh* 'dove'　*kuhãrĩh* 'cooks'

　　　　　　　　　　　malĩnĩh 'raspberry' (with longstem vowels)

The rule, however, seems to be optional as shown by the examples (quoted from Belić) cited in (8) above.[5]

We note also that the inflectional ending of the gen. sg. of certain feminine stems exhibits rising pitch:

(12)　*ženẽ* 'woman'　*lĩhẽ* 'garden'　*gorẽ* 'mountain'

We shall assume that there is a special rule that assigns a rising tone to this desinential vowel. This rule might conceivably be part of the rule mentioned above which assigns rising pitch to vowels followed by a sonorant which in turn is followed by a consonant or a word boundary.

---

[5] A retraction rule formally similar to (10) also appears to be operating in Modern Russian where it accounts for such accentual alternations as

　　ugla ∼ *ugal* 'corner'　　*uzla* ∼ *uz,il* 'knot'　　　*ugr,a* ∼ *ugar'* 'eel'
　　ugl,a ∼ *ugal'* 'coal'　　　*kruživa* ∼ *kruživ* 'lace'
　　bal,na ∼ *bol,in* 'ill'　　　*ravna* ∼ *rov,in* 'even'

I have discussed these cases in Halle (1971).

4. There is a special Štokavian dialect group, the so-called Slavonian dialects, which exhibits both types of "rising" tone, the one we find in the literary Štokavian dialects as well as the one in the Čakavian dialects. The Slavonian dialects have been studied in some detail by various scholars, including S. Ivšić, who first drew attention to them in 1911, and P. Ivić, who devoted a chapter to them in his *Die serbokroatischen Dialekte* I (Mouton, 1958).

(13) vrãtīm 'turn' (1st sg.)   vrátit (inf.)   nõž – nóža 'knife'
    tũrīt 'put' (3rd sg.)   túrit (inf.)   sačũvām 'keep' – čúvat (inf.)

To understand these examples we need to look at underlying forms of some of the forms just cited:

$$\begin{array}{cccc} +H & +H & +H & +H \\ vr\bar{a}ti+\bar{\imath}+m & vr\bar{a}ti+t & n\tilde{o}\check{z}+ъ & n\tilde{o}\check{z}+a \end{array}$$

We then see readily that the NEOACUTE rule will assign [+R] to the long vowel in the pre-H position. The TRUNCATION and JER DELETION rule will delete the last [+H] vowel in vrãtīm and nõž respectively but not in vrátit and nóža, leaving us with distinct output forms

$$vr\begin{bmatrix} \bar{a} \\ +R \\ +stress \end{bmatrix} t \begin{bmatrix} \bar{\imath} \\ -H \end{bmatrix} m \; vr \begin{bmatrix} \bar{a} \\ +R \\ +stress \end{bmatrix} t \begin{bmatrix} i \\ +H \end{bmatrix} t$$

$$n\begin{bmatrix} +\bar{o} \\ +R \\ stress \end{bmatrix} \check{z} \qquad n \begin{bmatrix} \bar{o} \\ +R \\ +stress \end{bmatrix} \check{z} \begin{bmatrix} a \\ +H \end{bmatrix}$$

i.e. we get acute ′ when a [+H] vowel follows; neoacute ˜ when it does not.[6]

5. We now turn to what is without doubt the most complicated of the prosodic systems found in the Slavic languages — that of Slovene. The handbooks tell us that Slovene has three types of accented

---

[6] The stress assignment rule of Slavonian is not perfectly clear to me as there seem to be a great many dialectal variations (see Ivić 1958, 285–290 and Ivšić 1912, 22–24). I shall assume here that the dialect from which the examples are drawn assigns stress to the penultimate vowel with [+H], if possible, and to the only [+H] otherwise.

vowel: one short, and two long. The short vowel is said to have always falling pitch; whereas there is a contrast between the two long vowels: one is rising and the other is falling. The rising pitch of Slovene is not to be identified with that of Štokavian; it is rather like the Noví neoacute.

(14)

	'linden'	'mountain'	'path'	'crayfish'	'man'	'column'
N	lípa	gǫ̑ra	stəzà	rȁk	mǫ̑ž	stəbə̀r
G	lípe	gǫre	stəzę̃	rȁka	mǫža	stəbrà
D	lípi	gǫ̑ri	stəzì	rȁku	mǫ̑žu	stəbrù
A	lípǫ	gǫrǫ̂	stəzǫ̇	rȁka	mǫža	stəbə̀r
I	lípǫ	gǫrǫ̃	stəzǫ̃	rȁkom	mǫ̑žem	stəbrǫ̀m
L	lípi	gǫ̑ri	stəzì	rȁku	mǫ̑žu	stəbrù
N	lípe	gǫre	stəzę̇	rȁki	mǫžjȩ̃	stəbrȉ
G	lȋp	gǫrã	stəzã	rákǫv	mǫ̑ž	stəbrǫ̃v
D	lípam	gǫràm	stəzàm	rȁkǫm	mǫžȩ̃m	stəbrǫ̀m
A	lípe	gǫrę̂	stəzę̂	rȁke	mǫžę̂	stəbrę̀
I	lípami	gǫràmi	stəzàmi	rȁki	mǫžmĩ	stəbrĩ
L	lípah	gǫràh	stəzàh	rȁkih	mǫžȩ̃h	stəbrȩ̃h

As shown in the examples in (15) below, the stress in Slovene words is placed on the same vowel as in Standard Štokavian rather than as in the Noví dialect:

(15)
Slovene   žȩ̃na 'woman'   kljúča 'key'   člǫ̑vȩk 'human being'
Štokavian žèna   kljúča   čòvek
Noví   žena   kljūčà   čovȉk

I propose therefore that Slovene has a STRESS ASSIGNMENT rule that, like the rule in Standard Štokavian, assigns stress to the penultimate vowel with [+H] if possible.[7]

There is, however, one fundamental difference between Slovene and Standard Štokavian. In Standard Štokavian nouns such as lȉpa which belong to the ACUTE category — i.e. which receive [+H] on the stem vowel by the H ASSIGNMENT rule — have "falling" tones

---

[7] The location of stress in circumflex words—i.e. in words to which he H ASSIGNMENT rule does not apply—is somewhat different in Slovene and will be briefly discussed below [cf. rule (19) and discussion there].

on this vowel; in Slovene, on the other hand, as shown in (14) the tone in these forms is usually "rising". In order to account for this difference we shall assume that in Slovene words with acute stems the H ASSIGNMENT rule places [+H] not on the stem vowel but on the next syllable, e.g.,

$$\begin{array}{ccc} +\text{H} & +\text{H} & +\text{H} \\ l\overline{\imath}p+a \text{ 'linden'} & rak+a \text{ 'crayfish'} & d\bar{e}klic+a \text{ 'girl'} \end{array}$$

Subsequent to this the H DISTRIBUTION rule applies and converts these strings to

$$\begin{array}{ccc} +\text{H}+\text{H} & +\text{H}+\text{H} & +\text{H}+\text{H} \\ l\overline{\imath}p+a & rak+a & d\bar{e}klic+a \end{array}$$

It is a well-known fact that in Serbo-Croatian acute stem vowels are always short, whereas circumflex stem vowels maintain distinctive length, which is also maintained in the stem vowels of oxytone stems. In terms of the rule system developed here this suggests that for Serbo-Croatian a rule should be postulated which applies before H DISTRIBUTION and shortens vowels marked [+H] by the H ASSIGNMENT rule. While such a shortening rule is appropriate for Serbo-Croatian, it does not seem justified for Slovene. To see this consider how we would account for the Slovene forms *rȁk* (nom. sg.) and *lȋp* (gen. pl.). If underlying representations are postulated that correspond to the etymology, we should get long vowels in both words.

$$\begin{array}{cc} r\bar{a}k+\text{ъ} & l\bar{\imath}p+\text{ъ} \\ +\text{H} & +\text{H} \end{array}$$

If there is a shortening rule in the grammar, this would normally be expected to apply to the stem vowel in both words as both words are acute. But this does not conform to the facts; in *rȁk* the vowel is short; in *lȋp* it is long. We should, therefore, assume that there is no shortening rule in Slovene; instead of that the respective words appear in the lexicon with distinctive length:

$$\begin{array}{cc} rak+\text{ъ} & l\bar{\imath}p+\text{ъ} \\ +\text{H} & +\text{H} \end{array}$$

The rules developed to this point will locate the stress in its proper position in the Slovene words under discussion. They do not account, however, for the fact that the stem vowel in the oblique case forms of *răk* is long (e.g. *rāka* gen. sg.) nor for the different tones on the stem and desinential vowels in (14). To account for the long vowel in the oblique case forms we postulate a special LENGTH rule that lengthens stressed vowels in nonfinal syllable [cf. (16) below]. The vowel [ə] appears always as short: this can be captured either by restricting the LENGTH rule or by adding a special rule to the NEUTRALIZATION and REDUCTION rules. Since nothing of relevance to the topic under discussion hinges on this decision I shall assume that the LENGTH rule is limited to vowels other than ə, a fact which I capture by the asterisk on the symbol V*:

(16) LENGTH
$$\begin{bmatrix} V^* \\ +\text{stress} \end{bmatrix} \rightarrow [+\text{long}]/[X\underline{\quad}C_0VY]$$

As a consequence of this rule the only position where stressed short vowels can be found in Slovene is the last syllable of the word.

The question of the tone features in Slovene is to be discussed next. Slovene has both rising and falling tones on stressed long vowels, whereas stressed short vowels have falling tone only.

The rising tone in Slovene is like that of the Noví dialect. It is found, however, not only in words that are cognate to the Noví words with rising pitch but also in words that are cognate to the Štokavian words with rising tone [cf. (15)], though as noted above the Slovene rising tone is phonetically a totally different phenomenon. We shall assume therefore that Slovene has a special rule assigning the feature [+R] to stressed long vowels in position before a vowel with [+H].

(17) RISE
$$\begin{bmatrix} V^* \\ +\text{stress} \end{bmatrix} \rightarrow [+\text{H}]/\left[X\underline{\quad}C_0\begin{bmatrix} V \\ +\text{H} \end{bmatrix}Y\right]$$

(In view of the LENGTH rule there is no need to restrict RISE to long vowels, but ə must be excluded.)

We observe immediately the formal similarity between the LENGTH rule (16) and the RISE rule (17). Both apply to stressed vowels other than ə in nonfinal syllables of a word. This suggests that the two rules should be ordered next to each other so that it should be possible to coalesce them into a schema with the help of the notational conventions of our theory. We shall not do it here since the RISE rule will undergo considerable modifications as the discussion proceeds. It suffices to note for our purposes that the two rules can be ordered adjacent to one another. If it is now assumed that the two rules follow the STRESS rule, forms such as *rãka*, with rising tone on the stem vowel, are readily explained.

The falling tone in Slovenian is found on stressed vowels when these are in the last syllable of the word. As noted above, in view of the LENGTH rule this is the only position where stressed vowels can be short. Moreover, because of the RISE rule falling tone can appear on long vowels only when the next vowel is not [+H], or if there is no vowel following. We shall assume then that FALLING is simply the term used to describe the quality of a stressed vowel that is not followed by a vowel marked [+H], and like Standard Štokavian, Slovene will have no special rule assigning the feature [+falling tone] to some stressed vowel.

These preliminaries out of the way, we now must consider more carefully the tonal features of the stem vowels in the declension of *lïpa* and *rằk*. We have proposed above that in both declensions the H ASSIGNMENT rule places [+H] on the desinence. We should therefore expect, in general, rising tones on the stem vowel. An examination of (14) reveals, however, that there are quite a number of forms where the stem vowel has falling tone. These must now be explained.

The appearance of falling tone in the nom. sg. *rằk* presents no difficulty as soon as it is realized that this form has a jer as its desinence. Since this jer is deleted before stress is assigned the stressed stem vowel in these forms can never be subject to the RISE rule and hence the forms will appear with falling stress in the output.

To account for the falling tone in the instr. sg. and gen. pl. of *lïpa* and in the loc. sg., gen. pl., instr. pl., loc. pl. of *rằk* we must add a rule to the grammar. A straightforward solution is provided by a METATONY rule that in these cases changes [+H] in the last syllable of the word to [−H]; for example,

$$\begin{array}{cc} +H+H & +H-H \\ lïp+\bar{o} & \rightarrow \quad lïp+\bar{o} \end{array}$$

We order this rule after the STRESS rule and before the RISE rule. Formally the rule might then read as

(18) METATONY-1

$$V \rightarrow [-H] / [X\underline{}C_0] \left\{ \begin{array}{l} \text{instr. fem. sg.} \\ \text{instr. masc. pl.} \\ \text{loc. masc. pl.} \\ \vdots \end{array} \right\}$$

Since the RISE rule follows METATONY, the former cannot apply in the cases under discussion, and these forms will appear in the output with falling tone as required.

Consider now the accentual patterns in the circumflex stems exemplified in (14) by *stəbə̀r, mô̧ž, gǫ̃ra, stəzà*. We note that in stems with *ə* as stem vowels the stress goes on the second syllable. Many of the forms of nouns with a full vowel in the stem also show stress on the second syllable. Moreover, forms with and without prepositions such as *gǫrô̧* but *nagô̧ro, gǫrȩ̂* but *nagô̧re* provide further support for the proposal that in circumflex words stress goes on the second syllable. The major exceptions to this rule are forms with a full stem vowel such as *gǫ̃ra, gǫ̃ri, mô̧žu*, all of which end with a short vowel. These forms require special treatment which cannot be discussed here. (I intend to deal with these forms in a subsequent publication.) Once these forms are excluded from consideration, the circumflex stems can all be said to be subject to (19):[8]

(19) CIRCUMFLEX STRESS rule

$$V \rightarrow \begin{bmatrix} +\text{stress} \\ +H \end{bmatrix} / [C_0VC_0\underline{}X]$$

Given the above discussion of the conditions that determine falling tone on stressed vowels we should expect falling tones in all forms of circumflex nouns. An examination of the paradigms of *gǫ̃ra, stəzà, mô̧ž*, and *stəbə̀r* in (14), however, shows that we get rising tone on the desinences precisely in those cases where in the acute paradigms of *rȁk* and *lĭpa* the stem vowel has falling in place of the expected rising tone [cf. rule (18)]. For convenience we repeat in (20) below

---

[8] I assume that (19) follows and is disjunctive with respect to the stress rules that apply to "acute" forms; i.e. to forms that contain a vowel marked [+H] by the H ASSIGNMENT rule. The rule (19) as stated supplies not only stress but also high tone ([+H]). This is required in order to insure the correct falling tone in such forms as *gǫrô̧ možâ gorâmi*. It gains additional support in that it allows us to combine rules (18) and (20) into a single rule (see discussion at end of section 5).

those case forms where acute nouns have falling tone on the stem
and circumflex nouns have rising tone on the desinence:

(20) instr. sg. fem.   *lîpo*   *gǫrǫ̃*   *stəzo*
      instr. pl. masc.   *râki*   *mǫžmĩ*   *stəbrĩ*
      loc. pl. masc.   *râkih*   *mǫžẽh*   *stəbrẽh*

In view of falling tone on the stem vowel in the loc. sg. *râku* it might have been expected that there would be a rising tone also on the desinence in *mǫ̂žu* and *stəbrù*. We recall, however, that rising tones can appear only on long vowels. Since the loc. sg. desinence has a short vowel, the absence of a rising tone in these forms is not a counterexample; it is rather a correct consequence of the fact that all short vowels must be $[-R]$.

To account for the facts illustrated in (20), it would appear, therefore, that the grammar must include a rule which assigns $[+R]$ to the stressed vowel in certain case forms of nouns with circumflex stems. In order to characterize uniquely the environment where the rule is to apply we recall that in nouns with circumflex stems the stressed vowel is the only vowel in the word that is $[+H]$. We provisionally formulate this rule as in (21):

(21) METATONY-2

$$V \rightarrow [+R] / [X\_\_\_C] \left\{ \begin{array}{l} \text{instr. fem. sg.} \\ \text{instr. masc. pl.} \\ \text{loc. masc. pl.} \end{array} \right\}$$

The solution that we are thus forced to by closely hugging the phonetic ground is not particularly attractive. By including both (18) and (21) in our solution we are stating in effect that two unrelated phonetic processes (the lowering of high pitch and the assignment of "rising" tones) take place in the same, highly idiosyncratic environment. Moreover, by adopting this solution we are giving up the interesting restriction proposed by Nancy Woo that "dynamic" tones such as "rising" or "falling" are not part of the universal feature framework and are always to be viewed as surface phenomena. An alternative solution seemed, therefore, highly desirable.

Our problem is to find a common denominator for the two processes represented in the rules (18) and (21). Suppose that "rising" pitches are basically "low" level tones, and that the rise in pitch that we perceive is due to a return of the voice from the "low" pitch inherent in the stressed vowel to the average pitch of the utterance. If this idea is correct, then rule (21) should assign to the word final vowel instead of a "rising" tone, a low — below normal pitch — tone which we shall designate here by the feature [+L]. Rule (21) would then be rewritten as in (22).

(22) METATONY

$$V \rightarrow \begin{bmatrix} +L \\ -H \end{bmatrix} / [X \underline{} C_0 \begin{Bmatrix} \text{instr. fem. sg.} \\ \text{instr. masc. pl.} \\ \text{loc. masc. pl.} \\ \vdots \end{Bmatrix}$$

We have added the feature [−H] on the right-hand side of the arrow to make explicit the fact that all "low" toned sounds are, by definition, [−H]. We see, moreover, that given this formulation, (22) is identical with (18) except for the appearance of [+L] on the right-hand side of the arrow. This distinction, however, has no effect on the functioning of the rule, for the sole purpose of METATONY rule (18) was to block the RISE rule (17) from applying to forms such as those in (20), and this purpose is achieved regardless of whether or not [+L] appears on the left-hand side of the arrow. Hence the single rule (22) can replace the two rules (18) and (21). In sum, if our assumption is correct that "rising" tones are surface manifestations of underlying "low" tones, then there is a single explanation — the assignment of a "low" tone to the last vowel in the word — for what on a more superficial view are two distinct processes: the replacement of "rising" tones by "falling" tones in one set of forms and the converse replacement of "falling" tones by "rising" in another set of forms.[9]

---

[9] If we let METATONY apply to the fem.sg. forms of the preterite participle we can readily account for the tone alternations found in different forms of this participle. We distinguish here three types of cases. In oxytone forms we get such alternations as

| bȉl (masc.) | bîla (fem.) | bȋlo (neuter) | 'beat' |
| mǭlčal | molčâla | molčâlo | 'be silent' |

To handle the acute and the circumflex stems the METATONY rule has to be extended so as to apply not only in the last syllable of the word, but also in the penultimate syllable:

In addition to allowing us to deepen our description in the manner outlined the proposal to view "rising" tones as surface reflexes of "low" level tones has also direct support in the phonetics of Slovene. We suggested above that the "rising" pitch perception is due to the fact that on such tones the voice returns from a lower than average pitch level to the average pitch. Similarly one might suppose that the "falling" pitch perception is due to the fact that the voice returns from a higher than average to the average ptch. In fact, a number of phoneticians, among them Olaf Broch and J. Toporišič, have felt that the above is a fairly accurate description of the state of affairs, at least, in some instances. Thus, after the usual comments about rising and falling tones of stressed vowels, Broch notes (p. 326) "... in gewöhnlicher rascherer Rede wird die Tonbewegung ausgeglichen. Zum Verlust der Tonbewegung scheint

$$V \rightarrow \begin{bmatrix} +L \\ -H \end{bmatrix} \begin{bmatrix} X \underline{\quad} C_0 \left(\begin{bmatrix} V \\ -H \end{bmatrix} C_0 \right) \end{bmatrix} \begin{Bmatrix} \text{fem. sg. pret. part.} \\ \text{instr. fem. sg.} \\ \text{instr. masc. pl.} \\ \text{loc. masc. pl.} \\ ... \end{Bmatrix}$$

With this extension we can readily account for the tonal alternations in acute verbs such as, e.g.

brâl (masc.)   *brăla* (fem.)   *brâlo* (neut.)   'take'

We assume that the H ASSIGNMENT rule assigns [+H] to the stem vowel. As a result we should get "falling" tone in all forms. The extended METATONY rule, however, applies to the fem. sg. forms and assigning to the penultimate vowel the features $\begin{bmatrix} +L \\ -H \end{bmatrix}$ provides the stem vowel in these forms with "rising" tone.

Forms with circumflex stems behave similarly to forms with acute stems, e.g.

kovâl   *kovăla*   *kovâlo*   'forge'
dajâl   *dajălă*   *dajâlo*   'give'

The CIRCUMFLEX STRESS rule (19) accounts for the falling tone on the second syllable of these forms. In the fem. form the extended METATONY rule converts the "falling" to "rising" tone in the manner outlined above.

The extended METATONY rule applies also in nouns with polysyllabic stems such as

dęklica (nom. sg.)   *dęklico* (instr. sg.)   'girl'

I hope to treat these metatonies in greater detail as well as other questions of Slovene accentology in a separate paper now in preparation. See also note 3.

besonders geneigt die Silbe unter ˜, die sehr häufig von steigendem zu annähernd ebenem Ton übergeht; aber auch unter ⌒ verliert die Silbe oft einen Teil der Tonbewegung, und zwar den letzten, tiefen Teil.

Auf diese Weise entsteht aber zwischen den gegebenen langen Silben ein neuer tonischer Gegensatz; wenn auch die fallende und die steigende Bewegung schwindet, so bleibt doch, mehr oder weniger deutlich, für ⌒, die relativ hohe Tonlage und für ˜ die relativ niedrige Tonlage, welche ursprünglich nur dem Anfangsteil des betreffenden Akzentes eigen war." And in a footnote on the same page Broch adds: "Bei meinem Untersuchungen bemerkte ich nicht selten bei einem meiner Gewährsmänner die Neigung für ⌒ einen höheren Ton als der der nichtakzentuierten Silben, für ˜ aber 'Tiefton', einen entsprechend tieferen zu gebrauchen: ⌒ = ‾‾; ˜ = __. Jedoch dürfte dies individuell sein und vielleicht durch den Wunsch hervorgerufen, dem Beobachter die Unter scheidung der Typen zu erleichtern."[10]

In other words, the assumption that rising and falling tones are surface reflexes of stationary low and high tones, respectively, not only leads to a greatly simplified system of phonological rules, but is apparently quite directly supported by the phonetic actualization of the tones in normal, unforced discourse.

6. In concluding I should like to recall the two theoretical considerations that have guided this study. I believe that the data reviewed support quite strongly Nancy Woo's proposal that "dynamic" tones are always phonetic phenomena of a superficial sort similar perhaps to such other phonetic surface phenomena as the vowel transition associated with particular consonantal points of articulation, the greater loudness of low vowels, or the tendency not to release a stop when the next segment is also a stop. What is significant here is that when "dynamic" tones were viewed in this very special way, the phonological processes of the dialects examined became more transparent, more understandable. Needless to say that what has been brought out here is far from conclusive, but as a step towards establishing Woo's hypothesis it is surely not negligible.

The second hypothesis of importance was Roman Jakobson's insight that Slavic accentual phenomena are best viewed as deriv-

[10] I have replaced Broch's diacritic mark ″ by ˜ to make it consistent with the usage of the rest of this article.

(24) Summary of rules discussed

	Russian	Štokavian	Novi	Slavonian	Slovene
	H ASSIGNMENT	H ASSIGNMENT	H ASSIGNMENT	H ASSIGNMENT	H ASSIGNMENT
	H DISTRIBUTION	H DISTRIBUTION	H DISTRIBUTION	H DISTRIBUTION	H DISTRIBUTION
			NEOACUTE	NEOACUTE	NEOACUTE
	VOWEL TRUNCATION	VOWEL TRUNCATION	VOWEL TRUNCATION	VOWEL TRUNCATION	VOWEL TRUNCATION
			RETRACTION		
	JER DELETION	JER DELETION	JER DELETION	JER DELETION	JER DELETION
	JER LOWERING	JER LOWERING	JER LOWERING	JER LOWERING	JER LOWERING
Assign stress in forms with H	to last H	to penult H / to last H	to last H	to penult H / to last H	to penult H / to last H
Assign stress in forms without H (circumflex)	to first syllable	to first syllable	to first syllable	to first syllable	to second syllable / to first syllable
	NEUTRALIZATION	NEUTRALIZATION	NEUTRALIZATION		METATONY
					LENGTH
					RISE

ing from a stage in which the language resembled a simple "terrace tone" language like Japanese. While Jakobson understood his proposal primarily in diachronic terms I hope that the discussion above has shown that the conception holds true also synchronically, where derivation is understood in the normal sense of generative phonology. As in the case of the first hypothesis the significant fact is not that by using a particular approach a body of data can be catalogued, but rather that when this approach is used a host of complicated facts appear to fall neatly into place. Several examples have been cited in the body of the paper, but perhaps none is as impressive as the clear picture of relatedness among different dialects which emerges when we juxtapose, as in (24), the ordered sets of rules that had to be postulated to handle the particular data of the different dialects that have been studied here.

Massachusetts Institute of Technology

REFERENCES

Belić, A.
    1909 "Zametki po čakavskim govoram", *Izvestija otd. russkogo jazyka i slovesnosti Imperatorskoj Akademii Nauk* 14 (2), 181–266.

Broch, O.
    1911 *Slavische Phonetik* (Carl Winter, Heidelberg).

Chomsky, N. and M. Halle
    1968 *The Sound Pattern of English* (Harper and Row, New York).

Coats, H. S.
    1970 "Word Stress Assignment in a Generative Grammar of Russian", unpublished Doctoral dissertation, University of Illinois, Urbana, Illinois.

Halle, M.
    1970 "A Note on the Accentual Patterns of the Russian Nominal Declension", R. Jakobson and S. Kawamoto, eds., *Studies in General and Oriental Linguistics* (TEC Company Ltd., Tokyo), 167–174.

Halle, M.
    1971 "A Minor Accentual Rule of Contemporary Standard Russian". L. L. Hammerich, et. al., eds., *Form and Substance* (Akademisk Forlag, Copenhagen), 211—219.

Ivić, P.
    1958 *Die serbokroatischen Dialekte I* (Mouton, The Hague).

Ivšić, S.
    1913 "Današńi posavski govor", *Rad Jugoslavenske Akademije znanosti i umjetnosti* (Zagreb) 196, 124-204; 197, 9–138.

Jakobson, R.
1963 "Opyt fonologičeskogo podxoda k istoričeskim voprosam slavjanskoj akcentologii", *American Contributions to the Fifth International Congress of Slavists* (Mouton, The Hague), 153-178.

Jakobson, R.
1965 "Information and Redundancy in the Common Slavic Prosodic Pattern", *Symbolae Linguisticae in Honorem Georgii Kurylowicz* (Polska Akademia Nauk, Wrocław-Warszawa-Kraków), 145-151.

Lehiste, I. and P. Ivić
1963 *Accent in Serbocroatian* (= *Michigan Slavic Materials* 4) (Department of Slavic Languages and Literatures, Ann Arbor).

Lightner, T. M.
1965 "Segmental Phonology of Modern Standard Russian", unpublished Doctoral dissertation, MIT, Cambridge, Mass.

Lunt, H. G.
1966 "An Attempt at a Generative Description of the Slovene Verb", in R. L. Lenček, *The Verb Pattern of Contemporary Standard Slovene* (Otto Harrassowitz, Wiesbaden), 133-187.

Svane, G. O.
1958 *Grammatik der slowenischen Schriftsprache* (Rosenkilde und Bagger, Copenhagen).

Toporišič, J.
1968 "Liki slovenskih tonemov", *Slavistična Revija* 16, 315-393.

Woo, N. H.
1969 "Prosody and Phonology", unpublished Doctoral dissertation, MIT, Cambridge, Mass.

Zaliznjak, A. A.
1967 *Russkoe imennoe slovoizmenenie* (Nauka, Moscow).

ON 'HAVE' AND 'BE' LANGUAGES

(A Typological Sketch)

ALEXANDER V. ISAČENKO

1. In recent years, the manifold structural (syntactic and semantic) interrelations between the verbs *have* and *be* have been the subject of numerous stimulating and challenging studies.[1] The attention of most investigators is focused on what is usually called the 'possessive' relation and on its surface manifestations in different languages. A hypothesis has been formulated by John Lyons according to which "in many, perhaps in all, languages existential and possessive constructions derive (both synchronically and diachronically) from locatives".[2] The evidence upon which this hypothesis is based is taken from Latin and some modern West European languages. Languages in which the verb *have* either does not exist at all or is restricted in its use are quoted in isolated and trivial examples and interpreted within a ready framework of semantic and syntactical relations which are said to be 'universal'. In a recent study on *having* and *being* in Estonian Ilse Lehiste adduced ample evidence for the fact that a variety of constructions in which English would use the verb *have* are implemented in Estonian by constructions using the verb *be*.[3]

---

[1] W. S. Allen, "Transitivity and Possession", *Language* 40 (1964), 337-343. — E. H. Bendix, *Componential Analysis of General Vocabulary: The Semantic Structure of a Set of Verbs in English, Hindi, and Japanese* (Bloomington: Indiana University Press and The Hague: Mouton, 1966). — E. Benveniste, "'Être' et 'avoir' dans leurs fonctions linguistiques", *BSL*, LV (1960), 113-134. — C. H. Kahn, "The Greek Verb 'to be' and the Concept of Being", *Foundations of Language* 2 (1966), 245-265. — J. Kuryłowicz, "Les temps composés du roman ", *Prace Filologiczne* 15 (1931), 448-453 [Reprinted in *Esquisses linguistiques* (Wrocław and Kraków, 1960)]. — I. Lehiste, " 'Being' and 'Having' in Estonian", *Foundations of Language* 5 (1969), 324-341. — J. Lyons, "A Note on Possessive, Existential and Locative Sentences", *Foundations of Language* 3 (1967), 390-396.

[2] J. Lyons, *op. cit.*, 390.

[3] I. Lehiste, *op. cit.*

All Indo-European and Finno-Ugric languages have the verb *be*, but only some of them also use a verb corresponding to *have*. The absence of the verb *have* or its restricted use in some languages has far reaching consequences for their entire semantic and syntactical structure. *Be* and *have* constructions form the kernel of syntax, and it is by no means unjustified to polarize modern European languages into *have*-languages (H-languages) and *be*-languages (B-languages). The former include English, German, Dutch and the other Germanic languages, French and the other Romance languages, Czech, Slovak and Serbo-Croatian as well as Lithuanian. The latter include Finnish, Estonian, Hungarian and Russian, as well as Latvian.[4] Polish, Ukrainian and Belorussian seem to be in a state of transition from B-languages to H-languages.

2. It is well known that Indo-European was a B-language and that the verbal stems **es-* and **bhū-* very early merged into a suppletive paradigm preserved in most historically attested IE idioms. It is also known that verbs meaning 'have' are secondary acquisitions in all IE languages and that such verbs stem from transitive verbs with the general meaning 'to hold, to grasp'. This is true of Greek ἔχειν 'to have' (originally 'to hold'),[5] of Latin *habēre* which is related to *capere* 'to catch, get hold of';[6] it is true of Germanic **habai-* which yielded ME *have*, Germ *haben* and is not related to Latin *habēre*, but to Goth *hafjan*, ME *heave*, Germ *heben*;[7] the Slavic verb **jьměti* 'to have' (R *imét'/iméju*, Cz *míti/mám*, Slk *mat'/mám*, etc.) is formed from the root **jьm-* as attested in OCS *jęti* (from **jem-ti*) 'to take'. The semantic change 'take' → 'have' occurred in historical times in Spanish, where *tengo* 'I have' is derived from VLat *tenire* 'to hold'.[8]

---

[4] Cf. J. Marvan, "K otázkám kategorie slovesného spůsobu v současné lotyštině", *Acta Universitatis Carolinae — Philologica Slavica Pragensia* IV (1962), 254.
[5] Cf. E. Boisacq, *Dictionnaire étymologique de la langue grecque* (2nd ed.; Heidelberg–Paris, 1923), 302–303.
[6] Cf. A. Ernout and A. Meillet, *Dictionnaire étymologique de la langue latine* (Paris, 1932), 421–422.
[7] F. Kluge/W. Mitzka, *Etymologisches Wörterbuch der deutschen Sprache* (18th ed.; Berlin, 1960), 278.
[8] A brilliant presentation of the problem was given by A. Meillet in "Le développement du verbe avoir", *Antidôron J. Wackernagel* (1924), 9–13.

There is, of course, nothing metaphysical about H-languages and B-languages. The first European language to have introduced the verb *have* was Greek; other languages acquired the verb *have* in historical times and *have*-constructions are spreading at a steadily increasing rate, affecting the semantics of numerous 'relational' verbs in the central layers of the vocabulary. Since the 'possessive' relation is usually considered to be the most representative for the distinction between *have* and *be* constructions, we shall start our observations with the analysis of predicative "possessive" constructions in Russian.

3. According to John Lyons, "Russian possessives in predicate position are patently related to locatives".[9] In Russian constructions of the type *u A (est') B* the question whether they should be translated as *A has B* or *There is B near A* depends, according to Lyons, very largely upon whether *A* is a personal noun or not.[10] This assertion is at variance with observational adequacy. Take the following three sentences:

(1)   U Péti est' mašína 'Peter has a car'
(2)   Mašína u Péti 'The car is with/at Peter'
(3)   Mašína v garažé 'The car is in the garage'

The prepositional phrase in (2) is not identical with the prepositional phrase in (1), but in (3). Both *v garažé* and *u Péti* (in 2) may be labelled 'local' in a rather wide sense, but only *v garaže* is a locative proper, whereas *u Péti* (2) is adessive.[11] On the other hand,

---

[9] J. Lyons, *op. cit.*, 394.
[10] *Ibid.*
[11] An excellent semantic analysis of the preposition *u* in Russian is given by R. Mrázek and J. Brym in "Sémantika a funkce ruského genitivu s předložkou 'u'", *Sborník prací filosofické fakulty brněnské university* A-10 (1962), 99–118. Anyone working on problems related to ours should have read this paper. It is based on an unusually rich collection of examples, some of which are utilized in our presentation. The authors posit for Russian *u* a 'general meaning' as expressing a 'relation of a very close participation of something in something' (p. 101). They distinguish four contextual meanings: (1) ablative *(on zánjal u menjy dén'gi* 'he borrowed money from me'); (2) 'static local' *(on byl v gostjáx u Volódi* 'he was a guest at Volodja's'); (3) the meaning of 'appurtenance' and 'possession' *(syn u menjá účitsja v Prage* 'my son studies in Prague'), and (4) the 'implicational' (zřetelový) or 'limitational' meaning *(u sílnogo bessílnyj vsegdá vinovát* 'with the strong one, the feeble is always

the phrase *u Péti* in (1) is not interpreted as a 'locative'. The preposition *u* denotes a specific (and certainly not 'local') relation which for lack of a traditional term we shall label as 'relation of concern or implication'. Note that the difference between the possessive and the local (adessive) interpretation of the *u + Gen* construction depends upon whether the prepositional phrase stands in the topic position (as in 1), or in the comment position (as in 2).

Diachronically the relation of the 'implicational' preposition *u* with the adessive preposition *u* is very likely, but cannot be established by historical evidence. Slavic *u* is related to IE **ab* 'away' (as in the Latin verbal prefix *au-ferre* 'carry away' or in R *u-nesti* 'id.'). The original meaning of the preposition was clearly ablative. The semantic development 'ablative' → 'adessive' is difficult to follow historically. But synchronically, the 'implicational' *u* in Russian is homonymous with the adessive *u* (as in 2), causing, as we shall show, prepositional phrases *u + Gen* to be ambiguous in numerous instances.

In constructions with verbs other than 'be' the preposition *u* is interpreted as adessive, if the noun of the prepositional phrase is non-personal:

(4)   Lámpa stoít *u okná* 'The lamp stands by the window.'
(5)   Pétja žil *u vokzála* 'Peter lived near the railroad station.'
(6)   My vstrétimsja *u škóly* 'We shall meet near/at the school.'

If the noun of the prepositional phrase is personal, the adessive meaning is preserved in constructions with verbs other than *be* regardless of the topic/comment status of *u + A* which can often be translated into English by 'at A's place':

(7)   Pétja rabótaet *u arxitéktora* 'Peter works at/with an architect'
(8)   *U Péti* vstrečájutsja artísty 'Actors meet at Peter's place.'

Again, the topic/comment status of the prepositional phrase does not affect the adessive interpretation of the construction *u + Gen*.

---

guilty') *(ibid.)*. The 'ablative' meaning postulated by the authors can be easily included in the more general 'implicational' meaning, cf. *U menjá ukráli čemodán* 'I had a suitcase stolen'. The normal ablative preposition in Russian is *ot*.

4. There exists in Russian a variety of sentences traditionally called 'impersonal' which we prefer to label 'subjectless' or 'predicate-sentences'.[12] Since the verb *be* is deleted in the present, we shall symbolize this verb by E:

(9)   E Večer (Byl večer) '(It is) evening (was evening)'.
(9a) Segódnja E teplyj véčer 'Today (it is) a warm evening'.

We interpret the construction $E + NP$ in (9) as representing the predicate, the nominal phrase *večer* (or *tëplyj večer* 'a warm evening') being the predicate noun. A similar construction consists of E+ Adj (neuter sing.):

(10) E Véselo (Býlo véselo) '(It is) gay (was gay)'.

Such predicate-sentences may be expanded by various adverbials:

(10a) Tam vsegdá E véselo 'There always (it is) gay'.

Sentences of the type (10) may be expanded by adverbials consisting of the prepositional phrase $u + Gen$; they will always be interpreted as adessive:

(10b) U Péti vsegdá E véselo 'At Peter's it is always gay'.

---

[12] The problem of 'impersonal' sentences in Russian has been discussed in the framework of generative grammar by E. Klima, *IJSLP* VI (1963), 146-152. — R. Růžička, "O transformacionnom opisanii tak nazyvaemyx bezličnyx predloženij v sovremennom russkom literaturnom jazyke", *Voprosy jazykoznanija* 3 (1963), 22-31; V. Hrabě and P. Adamec, *Transformační syntax současné ruštiny*, mimeographed (Prague: by Charles University, 1969), 41-51. Recently, L. R. Micklesen has taken up the issue, utilizing some theoretical assumptions made by Katz and Postal for English. Impersonal surface constructions are considered by Micklesen to be produced by the deletion of a NON-ANIMATE nominal pro-form in the course of the derivational history, cf. "Impersonal Sentences in Russian", *American Contributions to the Sixth International Congress of Slavists* (The Hague: Mouton, 1969), preprint. While doubtlessly helping to explain some of the syntactical problems posed by impersonal surface constructions (such as the 'agreement' of the predicate with a NON-ANIMATE neuter singular 'subject'), the introduction of a deletable dummy does not really eliminate the difference between sentences which appear as 'personal' or 'impersonal' in their surface structures, since even in the deep structure there will remain the essential difference between sentences with non-deletable and with deletable subjects. In this paper we cannot go into the details connected with what we call 'predicate-sentences'.

But in sentences of the type (9) the prepositional phrase may be ambiguous:

(11) U Péti segódnja E koncért 'Peter has a concert tonight'.

The Russian sentence (11) is ambiguous in exactly the same way as is the corresponding English *have*-construction; it may mean:

(a) Peter has to perform in a concert tonight;
(b) Peter has to attend a concert as listener tonight;
(c) There is a concert at Peter's place tonight.

It is clear that the ambiguity of (11) in Russian is due to the polysemy of the constructions $u + Gen + E$. In the readings (a) and (b) the construction is interpreted as 'implicational', in (c) as adessive or local. In much the same way the predicate sentence *Sejčás vezdé E gripp* 'Now everywhere (there is) the flu' becomes ambiguous, if *vezdé* is replaced by a phrase $u + Gen$:

(12) Sejčás u Márkovyx E gripp.

In English, sentence (12) with implicational u would mean 'The Markovs have the flu now', but with the adessive u the reading would be 'There is flu at the Markovs'' implying that the Markovs themselves may not at all have the flu, but their cook is ill.

The difference between the implicational and the adessive meanings of $u + Gen$ is ultimately due to the presence of two different verbs in the underlying structure. If (9) has to be interpreted as 'The Markovs have the flu' (implicational relation), the symbol E stands for the attributive or 'copulative' *be*, cf. *U Márkovyx E véselo* 'At the Markovs' it is gay'. But if (9) is interpreted as 'There is the flu at the Markovs'', the symbol E stands for the existential *be* 'At the Markovs' there exists the flu'. In Russian these two meanings of the verb *byť* have to be distinguished. As was shown by Benveniste, the existential and the copulative meanings merged into one verb *be*.[13] If in Russian the different interpretation of the $u + Gen + E$ is due to different meanings of the verb *byť*, then from a synchronic point of view the prepositional phrase $u + Gen$ in both constructions can be said to be identical. Note that in Czech, a typical H-language, the two readings of (12) are formally distinguished:

[13] E. Benveniste, " 'Être' et 'avoir' ", 114–115.

(12a) Markovovi mají chrípku 'The Markovs have the flu'.
(12b) U Markovových mají chrípku 'At the Markovs' they have the flu'.

Characteristically, Russian *be*-constructions with an adjective in the predicate as in (10b) correspond in some H-languages to both *be* and *have* constructions:

(10b) G Bei Peter *ist es* schön (gemütlich) 'It is nice (cosy) at Peter's'.
   Cz U Petra *je* pěkno/*je to* pěkné (útulné).
(10c) G Peter *hat es* schön (gemütlich) 'id.'.
   Cz Petr *to má* pěkné (útulné).

Note that the 'situational' subject *es*/*to* of (10b) reappears as the complement of *have* in (10c). There be can little doubt that the constructions (10b) and (10c) are surface implementations of one and the same deep structure. However, the conversion of *be*-sentences into *have*-constructions of this type is limited to certain adjectives: there is no *Bei Peter ist es langweilig* 'At Peter's it is dull' → **Peter hat es langweilig*, Cz *U Petra je to nudné* → **Peter má to nudné*.

On the other hand, there exist in H-languages *have*-constructions with adjectives or adverbialized prepositional phrases without corresponding *be*-constructions:

(13) G Peter *hat es* eilig 'Peter is in a hurry'.
   Cz Petr *má to* naspěch.
(14) G Peter *hat es* nötig/notwendig 'Peter needs that'.
   Cz Petr *má to* zapotřebí.

In B-languages such as Russian there are no corresponding *have*-constructions *(*Petja iméet k spéxu)*. Dative + E constructions are used instead: *Mne E k spéxu* 'I am in a hurry', *Mne E núžno* 'I need' (see below 15.4).

The intimate relationship between Dative and u + Gen in Russian is evident, but the two are used in complementary distribution: Dative with adjectival predicates, u + Gen with nominal predicates.[14] Note the correspondence between the following *have*- and *be*- constructions:

---

[14] There are very few exceptions to this rule, cf. R *Emu E dvádcat let* 'He is twenty years old', but F *Il a vingt ans* 'He has twenty years'.

(15) F J'ai froid (chaud) 'I am cold (hot)'.
R Mne E xólodno (žárko).
(16) G Ich habe Angst 'I have a fear, I am scared'.
Cz Mám strach.
R Mne E strášno.

5. The evidence of Slavic historical syntax suggests that Common Slavic was a B-language. The numerous constructions with *iměti* which are to be found in OCS texts are without exception loan-translations from Greek constructions with ἔχειν.[15] The history of the penetration of the verb *jьměti* 'have' into the Slavic languages has to be written yet. In this article we can give only a brief sketch of the penetration of *iměti* into Russian.

All examples of *iměti* quoted by Sreznevskij *(Materialy* I, p. 1096) stem from Slavonian (Church Slavic) texts. In the Chronicles *iměti* occurs exclusively in phraseological units in combination with an abstract noun: *iměti mirъ, ljubovь, ratь, družbu, pravdu, serdce, lestь*.[16] In legal documents we find only *imati* + *Acc.* meaning 'to take, to receive'. The verb 'have' appears, in a curious Polish–Russian hybrid from *měti, měli* (P *mieć, mieli*) towards the end of the 15th century in the diplomatic correspondence of the Lithuanian Grand Prince Alexander, but it is used as a modal auxiliary meaning 'to have to'.[17] Ivan IV, who had a great gift of stylistic mimicry, uses *měti* (along with numerous other Polonisms) in his messages to S. Batory.[18] During the 15th century the Polonism *majetnostь* 'possession' is frequently used in Russian legal texts without, however, stimulating the use of *iměti* in the meaning of 'to possess'. Neither the *Paris Muscovite Glossary* of 1586, nor Richard James' *Russian–English Glossary* of 1618/1619, which are the most reliable sources of our knowledge about the vernacular of the period, mentions the verb *iměti*. It may be concluded *ex silentio* that *iměti* was not used in the vernacular. Curiously enough, the first examples of *iměti* occur in the quasi-vernacular dialogs which are added to Russian

---

[15] Cf. *Slovník jazyka staroslověnského* 13 (1966), 767–768.
[16] Cf. A. I. Hen'sors'kyj, *Halyc'ko-volyn'skyj litopys* (Kiev, 1961), 156, 163.
[17] O dočeri svoei, našoi velikoi knegini ... i o panjaxъ Greckogo zakonu, kotoryi byli měli pri nei měškati '... who had had to stay with her' (1493).
[18] ... oni čotyre zamki v zemli Lifljanskoj ... v storonu našu měli xotěli; ... otpravleny ot tebja byti měli (1581).

grammars published in the beginning of the 18th century by foreigners.[19]

The forms *iměti, iměju, imějusčij* appear with the mark 'Russian' in the anonymous dictionary of the first half of the 18th century ascribed to Tatiščev.[20] Under the influence of German and French, *iměť* penetrates into the language of the Russian educated elite in numerous phraseologisms and is firmly established in the literary language by the end of the 18th century. It takes another century until *iměť*-constructions begin to penetrate into the spoken language of the less educated speakers.

6. In Contemporary Standard Russian the verb *iměť* seems to be fully accepted. The dictionaries give a variety of usages of *iměť*. The bulk of the examples quoted in recent lexicographical sources

---

[19] Elias Kopijewitz quotes in his *Rukovedenie vъ grammatyku* (1706) only the rather fantastic sentence *Iměi sebě dobruju nočъ* 'have a good night' (p. D2). — In the *Anfangs-Gründe der Russischen Sprache* (1731), which is usually ascribed to V. E. Adodurov, the entire paradigm of the verb *iměť* is added to the paradigm of the verb *byť*. Both verbs are called *Verba Auxiliaria* (p. 42), which clearly speaks in favor of a non-Russian grammatical pattern.

The Swedish *Grammatica Russica* by Michael Groening (1750), which closely follows Adadurov's grammatical sketch, also contains the entire paradigm of *imětь* (p. 135). Far more interesting are the sentences quoted in the *Conversations* added to the grammar which seem to reproduce with a high degree of fidelity the spoken language of Russian merchants. We find the following idioms and constructions with *imětь* : *neiměju vremeni* 'I have no time' (232, 239, 249), *čestь iměju* 'I have the honor' (234), *Onъ iměetъ xorošej vidъ* 'He looks good', *Onъ iměetъ xorošej stanъ* 'He has a good figure' (248), *Vy nikakogo pesku neiměete* 'You have no sand' (250), *(Pokoj) položenie iměetъ izrjadnoe* '(The room) has an excellent situation' (253), *My iměemъ izrjadnyja kamorki* 'We have excellent rooms' (258), *neiměju oxoty* 'I do not feel like' (260), *Ja imělъ gorjačku* 'I had fever' (265), *Skolьko zarjadovъ poroxu vy iměete vъ svojemъ rožkě?* 'How many loads of powder do you have in your horn?' (268). There is only one *u + Gen* construction: *u menja očenь xorošija sukna* 'I have very good cloths'. Constructions with *iměť* are frequent in the *Šutlivyja i inyja gistorii*, added to the grammar and clearly translated from Western European sources: *Někotoroj Papa iměja nesnosnyj lomъ vъ kostjaxъ* 'A certain Pope having an unbearable ache in his bones' (283), *ja iměju prikazъ* 'I have the order' (*ib.*), etc. Some of the phrases seem to be ad hoc translations, e.g. *neimětь vremeni* (cf. *mne nekogda*), *Ja imělъ gorjačku* (cf. *U menja byla gorjačka*), *neiměju oxoty* (cf. *u menja net oxoty*). But these examples cannot be simply ignored.

[20] Cf. *Slovar' sovremennogo russkogo literaturnogo jazyka* 5 (1956), 298.

are phraseological units with *imét'* + *abstract noun* whose Western models are self-evident: *imet' čest'* 'have the honor', *i. sposóbnost'* 'have the aptitude, faculty', *i. talánt* 'have the talent', *i. sčást'e* 'have the luck', *i. ves* 'carry weight', *i. avtoritét* 'have the authority', *i. reputáciju* 'have the reputation'; *i. otnošenie* 'be related to', *i. vlijánie* 'have an influence', *i. vozmóžnost'* 'have the possibility', *i. ponjátie* 'have an idea (about)', *i. dérzost'* 'have the impudence', *i. terpénie* 'have the patience'; *i. délo s* 'have to do with' *(avoir affaire* or *avoir à faire)*, *i. mésto* 'take place, occur' *(avoir lieu)*, *i. slovo* 'have the floor', *i. uspéx* 'have success', *i. značénie* 'have significance', *i. namérenie* 'have the intention', etc. There are constructions with nouns denoting measures: *imét' dlinú* 'have the length of', *i. širinú* 'have the width of', *i. glubinú* 'depth'. The noun may stand in the instrumental in *imet' zadačéj* 'have for a task', *imet' célju* 'have for a target' (cf. G *zur Aufgabe, zum Ziele haben*, or their French equivalents). There even occur examples like *imet' 30 let* 'be 30 years old' (Fr *avoir trente ans*).[21] The verb *imet'* also combines with numerous non-abstract nouns such as *imet' dén'gi, dom, mašínu, druzéj* 'have money, a house, a car, friends'. All this creates the illusion that *imet'* in Russian has roughly the same range of usages as in German, French or English.

7. To the superficial observer the usage of *imet'* in CSR appears to be unlimited. However, numerous *u + Gen* constructions have not been replaced by *imét'* constructions (in cases where languages like English have only 'have' constructions), so that Russian has not really become a H-language. The existence of two parallel constructions in Russian leads many scholars to assume that they are freely interchangeable.

In a recent article R. Channon discussed the issue in the following way: there exist in Russian constructions of the type *U Ivána (est') mnógo knig* and *Iván iméet mnógo knig*. One would like to be able to say that these essentially synonymous constructions come from the same deep structure and that "they differ by a late rule which gives them different surface structures and introduces sty-

---

[21] *Ibid.*
[22] R. Channon, "On Passivization in Russian", *Studies Presented to Professor Roman Jakobson by his Students* (Cambridge, Mass., 1968), 54.

listic differences between them". Channon applies the concepts of Fillmore's 'case syntax' to Russian. The nominal phrase $u + Gen$ is labelled 'Dative' (meaning something like 'beneficient'), the 'possessed object' is called 'Objective' and is said to have the 'objective case marker RO' (= roditeľnyj, Genitive).

The verb *imeť* 'to have' arises from the combination of *byť* 'to be' with the objective case marker RO = roditeľnyj, Genitive. (The rule producing *imeť* must necessarily precede the rule which changes the objective RO into VI [= viniteľnyj, Accusative], since the objective after *imeť* undergoes the change; special rules are of course needed to account for the syntactic peculiarities of numerals.) Thus, where the dative phrase [the $u + Gen$ phrase] is chosen as the subject, the objective phrase remains and retains its case marker, and the verb *imeť* arises from *byť* + RO (of an objective) after a noun phrase. Where the objective is chosen as the subject, it no longer follows *byť* and its case marker RO is deleted, causing *byť* to remain. The essential difference here between Russian and English is that Russian allows either noun phrase to become the subject, while English requires that in such sentences the dative be the subject. These two utterences, then, have the same deep structure, which accounts for their identity of meaning, and they differ substantively only in the choice of which noun phrase is to be the subject. All other differences stem automatically from that one.[23]

Probably not all linguists will consider the above discussion to represent the optimal explanation of the obvious affinity between the two constructions. Particulary the 'derivation' of *imét* from *byť* + *Gen* strikes one as rather counter-intuitive. The semantic and syntactic relationship between 'possessive' *be* and *have* constructions has been known for about fifty years[24] and has been discussed in numerous articles since. 'Case syntax' describes certain syntactic rearrangements which take place, if a particular noun phrase is 'chosen for subject'. But the linguistically relevant question is this: What makes the speaker choose a particular phrase as a subject? Is the speaker free eto make his choice spontaneously or is he restricted by certain properties of the noun phrases involved? Is it really true that in this particular case the *byť* and *imét* constructions differ from each other only 'stylistically'? Before answering these questions, we have to make several factual remarks.

[23] R. Channon, "On Passivization in Russian", 54.
[24] See footnotes 1 and 8. See also H. Safarewiczowa, "Oboczność *ja imeju* i *u menja est* w języku rosyjskim dziś i dawniej", *Prace komisji językoznawstwa*, Nr 3 (Wrocław — Warszawa — Kraków, 1964).

Channon's assumptions are based on inadequate observational data. Like the majority of scholars who adduce only the most trivial examples to illustrate the 'situation in Russian', Channon ignores the following facts:

(1) There are numerous non-phraseological 'possessive' *u + Gen* constructions in Russian which cannot be converted into *imét'* constructions, e.g. *U negó xoróšee nastroénie* 'He is in a good mood' → **On iméet xoróšee nastroénie.*

(2) There are numerous non-phraseological 'possessive' *imet'* constructions which cannot be converted into *u + Gen* constructions, e.g. *Kniga iméet mnógo illjustrácij* 'The book has many illustrations' → **U knigi (est') mnogo illjustracij.*

(3) The element *est'* in *u + Gen* constructions is not optional, as seems to follow from its being put between brackets by Channon.

As for the 'stylistic' differences between *u + Gen* and *imét'* constructions, the situation is rather complicated. In a great number of cases the two constructions are stylistically neutral and thus interchangeable, especially in the spoken language. The domain of the *imét'* constructions seems to be newspaper Russian and theoretical prose, while *u + Gen* prevails in colloquial Russian and in fiction. We do not, however, possess reliable data on the relative frequency and stylistic distribution of the two types of construction in CSR. Yet, in numerous cases, there is an appreciable difference: certain *imét'* constructions are felt to be 'less idiomatic' than the corresponding *u + Gen* constructions. Purists attribute them to German or Yiddish background and 'non-idiomatic' *imet'* constructions are frequently identified as typical for 'Odessite' Russian.[25] The 'non-idiomatic' flavor of *imét'* constructions is also utilized as a conventional device to characterize the Russian spoken by 'Western' foreigners.[26] All this deserves further investigation.

---

[25] This refers predominantly to constructions with *imét' + Infinitive*, e.g. *Čto vy iméete pred"javit'?* 'What can you produce (as evidence)?', a syntactical loan borrowing from Germ *Was haben Sie vorzuweisen?*

[26] Here are some samples of Russian sentences uttered by the 'German spy' Herr Silber in a mystery story 'Tajnik' currently published in the magazine *Ogonek* (1970, number 6, p. 30):

— ... Vilgel'm Pik i Maks Rejman tože *est'* moi sootečestvenniki. Ja *budu* nadejat'sja, čto frejlejn *imeet* xorošuju pamjat' ...

— To *est'* malen'koe preuveličenie. Ja *imeju* skromnyj bagaž znanij ...

— To *est'* prijatnoe sovpadenie. Ja *imeju* pros'bu vašego papy ... pri-

8. In Russian, as in many other languages, there are several meanings connected with the verb 'to be'.[27] In this context we are interested in the following three meanings: (A) the existential *byt́;* (B) the 'locational' *byt́*, and (C) the 'attributive' or 'copulative' *byt́*. The semantic difference is quite obvious, since each of the three meanings can be implemented by different quasi-auxiliary verbs. The semantic difference also explains the difference in the construction of the corresponding negative sentences:

A. Existential

(17a) V reké *est́* rýby 'In the river there are fish'.
(17b) V reké *iméjutsja* rýby.
(17c) V reké *net* ryb 'In the river there are no fish'.

C. Attributive (copulative)

(18a) Kit E rýba/Kit est́ rýba 'The whale is a fish'.
(18b) *Kit javljáetsja rýboj.*
(18c) Kit *ne* E rýba/Kit *ne est́* rýba 'The whale is not a fish'.

There is no need to distinguish a special 'equational' meaning in Russian *(Pariž E stolica Francii* 'Paris is the capital of France').

---

vezti emu ... čto-nibud' ljubopytnoe iz žizni sovremennyx sovetskix pisatelej ...

The transformational rules which generate this kind of 'Russian as spoken by Germans' are very simple:

(a) Insert *est́* for the zero-form of the verb *byt́* in the present (Oni ne odinakovy → Oni ne *est́* odinakovy).

(b) Replace imperfective present forms by the periphrastic future (Ja nadejus' → Ja *budu* nadejatsja).

(c) Replace *u* + *Gen* constructions by *imet́* constructions (U menja est pros'ba → Ja *imeju* pros'bu).

(d) Replace the pronoun *èto* by *to* (Èto prekrasnyj tost → *To est́* prekrasnyj tost).

Characteristically, the grammar that converts correct German sentences into ungrammatic sentences as uttered by a Russian contains a rule by which the present tense forms of the auxiliary *sein* 'to be' are deleted. In German novels Russians would say *Ich hungrig* 'I am hungry', *Du Deutscher* 'You are a German'.

[27] Although the logicians distinguish a large number of different *be*-operators, there is no need for the linguist to distinguish all of them (cf. K. Berka, "Funkcii glagola 'byt' s točki zrenija sovremennoj formaľnoj logiki", in *Logiko-grammatičeskie očerki* [Moscow: Vysšaja škola, 1961], 160–180).

In many languages, 'existence' is firmly linked with the verb *be*, but this is by no means universal. In H-languages existence is often expressed by *have*, cf. F *il y a* literally 'there it has'. Among the Slavic languages existence is linked with *have* in SC *ima* 'there is' (and *nema* 'there is not'), B *ima/njama;* in Polish and Ukrainian only the negative forms show *have*, cf. P *niema*, U *nemaje*.

Russian, a B-language, uses 'impersonal' predicatives *esť* and *net/netu* which are historically connected with *be; esť* is no longer a finite verb form, but is historically the 3rd person sing. present of *byti; netu* is a contraction of **ne je tu* 'not is there'.

In some H-languages *have* constructions are equivalent to existential constructions with *give* or *be:*

(19a) Germ Es *gibt* (es *ist*) dort ein Theater 'There is a theater there'.
(19b) Sie *haben* dort ein Theater 'They have a theater there'.
(20a) Cz *Je* tam nový hotel 'There is a new hotel there'.
(20b) *Mají* tam nový hotel 'They have a new hotel there'.

English utilizes both 'be' and 'have' constructions in the 'existential' meaning.

The Russian 'possessive' constructions with $u + Gen + esť$ are usually considered as stylistical doublets of $u + Gen + zero$ form of *byť*. Mrázek and Brym point out that in such constructions the "very fact of possession" is stressed by *esť*.[28] Hrabě and Adamec consider the "relative stability of the possessive relation" to be one of the factors which condition the choice of *esť* or zero.[29] Without going into details here, we want to show that in certain contexts *esť* and zero constructions are far from being homonymous.

8.1. Compare the following two sentences:

(21) U negó esť sedýe vólosy 'He has gray hair'.
(22) U negó E sedýe vólosy 'He has gray hair'.

Note that the English sentence *He has gray hair* is ambiguous: It can mean 'He has *some* gray hair' as in (21), or '*(All of)* his hair is gray' as in (22). Sentences (21) and (22) would be ambiguous in Russian, if used in any other tense than the present, e.g. *U negó býli sedýe vólosy*. But in the present the semantic difference is marked

---

[28] R. Mrázek and J. Brym, "Semantika a funkce ruského genitivu", 110.
[29] V. Hrabě and P. Adamec, *Transformační syntax současné ruštiny* (Prague: Státní pedagogické nakladatelství [mimeographed edition], 1969), 45.

by the opposition *esť/zero*. The nominative noun phrase in (21) is marked as indefinite or 'partitive', the same noun phrase in (22) has no such mark. The semantic difference becomes even more prominent in the negative:

(21a) U negó *net* sedýx volós 'He has *no* gray hair'.
(22a) U negó ne sedýe vólosy 'He *does not have* gray hair'.

The indefinite meaning of *esť* appears whenever the 'possessed object' is implemented by a plural form: *(U negó esť) faľšívye zúby* 'He has some false teeth', *druz'já v Amérike* 'some friends in America', *dén'gi v bánke* 'some money in the bank', *originál'nye mysli* 'some original ideas', etc. In constructions without *esť* indefinite meaning is absent: *U negó faľšívye zúby* is equivalent to 'He wears dentures'. The appearance of quantifiers *(mnógo, néskoľko, málo, vse;* numerals) in the noun phrase effaces the indefinite meaning, cf. *U negó mnógo druzéj/U negó esť mnógo druzéj* 'He has many friends.

The same indefinite meaning is present, if the 'possessed object' is expressed by a *singulare tantum:*

(23) U negó esť starínnyja mébeľ 'He has (some) antique furniture'.
(24) U nego starínnyja mébeľ 'He has (only) antique furniture'.

If *toľko* 'only' is to be used, the construction will have the shape of (24): *U nego toľko pervoklássnyj továr* 'He has only first-class merchandise', and not **U nego esť toľko pervoklassnyj tovar.*

Names of diseases like *gripp* 'flu' or physical states such as *žar* 'fever', *temperatúra* 'temperature' are *singularia tantum*. Therefore the difference between indefinite and non-indefinite meaning can be expressed in the present:

(25) U negó *esť* žar 'He has *some* fever'.
(26) U negó E žar 'He has fever, he is feverish'.

These sentences are correlated with the negative sentences

(25a) U negó *net* žará 'He has *no* fever'.
(26a) U negó E ne žar, on prósto razgorjačílsja 'He does not have fever, he is simply heated up'.

8.2 The opposition of the *esť/zero* constructions is interpreted in a very specific manner if it refers to parts of the wardrobe. Zero constructions refer to the part of wardrobe actually being worn:

(27) U neë nóvye botínki 'She has (wears) new shoes'.

On the other hand, *est'* constructions of this type refer to mere 'possession':

(28) U neë *est'* nóvye botínki, no oná ix ne nósit 'She has new shoes, but does not wear them'.[30]

The assumption that *u* + *Gen* and *imét'* constructions are derived from the same deep structure in no way accounts for the differences between *est'* and *zero*. Even if it were possible to transform the sentences (21)–(28) without violating Russian 'idomaticity', the semantic differences discussed in 8.1 and 8.2 would be lost.

9. The proper domain of idiomatic *imet'* constructions are sentences of the type 'Personal noun + *imet'* + Abstract noun'. But even here there are important constraints; not every abstract noun appearing in *have* constructions in H-languages has its counterpart in Russian. The equivalent of 'I had a dream' is not *Ja imel son, but

(29) U menja byl son.

In much the same way the abstract nouns *predčúvstvie* 'misgiving', *xorósee nastroénie* 'good mood', *zdoróvyj vid* 'healthy look', *želúdočnoe rasstrójstvo* 'indigestion', *góre* 'sorrow', *nesčást'e* 'misfortune', *stolknovénie s načal'stvom* 'confrontation with the authorities' and many others are not optionally convertible into *imet'* constructions. It is not likely that such constructions should be considered phraseological units. There seems to exist some common semantic denominator which excludes *imet'* constructions in these cases. Unfortunately it is impossible to elaborate on this problem here.

Be this as it may, the attempt to reduce all *imet'* and *u* + *Gen* constructions to a common deep structure and to differentiate them 'by a late rule' proves unsuccessful. It certainly does not account for the lack of optional convertibility of the sentences quoted above.

---

[30] For a more detailed discussion see A. V. Isačenko, "Sloveso 'mat' v ruštine a čo s tým súvisí", *Ruština v škole* I (1948–1949), 11–34; P. Adamec, "K ekvivalentům sloves 'býti' a 'míti' v ruštině", *Rusko-české studie*, in *Sborník Vysoké školy pedagogické v Praze, Jazyk a literatura (Kopeckij-Festschrift)* II (1960), 205 ff.

10. Let us turn now to Russian *imet'* constructions where the 'possessor' is an inanimate noun:

(30) Kvartíra iméet vánnuju 'The apartment has a bathroom'.

Such sentences are not convertible into *u* + *Gen* constructions: it is impossible to say **U kvartiry (est') vannaja*. If a *be* construction is to replace a sentence of the type (30), only locative noun phrases can be used:

(30a) *V kvartíre* est'vánnaja 'In the apartment there is a bathroom'.
(30b) *V kvartíre* E vánnaja.

The difference between the last two sentences lies in the use of existential *byt'* in (30a) and of attributive *byt'* in (30b).

Here again the assumption of an optional convertibility of *have* and *be* constructions in Russian proves wrong. The locative phrase is not a 'Dative' (or beneficiary).

On the other hand, not every sentence of the type (30a) can be converted into an *imet'* construction, cf. *V sadú est' stárye derév'ja* 'In the garden there are old trees' → **Sad iméet stárye derév'ja*.

The invariant grammatical meaning of the reflexive morpheme *-sja* in Russian is the explicit signalization of intransitivity.[31] The addition of *-sja* to any transitive verb causes the verb to become intransitive:

(31a) Knigotorgóvec prodaët knígi 'The bookseller sells books' (trans.)
(31b) Kníga xorošó prodaët*sja* 'The book sells well' (intrans.).

Transitive verbs such as *kusát'* 'bite', *deržát'* 'hold', *varít'* 'cook' are regularly intransitivized by *-sja*, cf. *Sobáka kusáetsja* 'The dog bites', *Kráska déržitsja* 'The paint is holding', *Sup váritsja* 'the soup is cooking'.

If we interpret transitivity as the ability of a verb to take an accusative object, then Russian *imet'* is a transitive verb.[32] Accord-

---

[31] Cf. A. V. Isačenko, *Grammatičeskij stroj russkogo jazyka v sopostavlenii s slovackim* II (Bratislava, 1960), 349–354.

[32] E. Benveniste considers the verb *have* to be a 'pseudo-transitive'. Since *have* does not refer to a 'process', it does not 'affect' or 'modify' the object (" 'Être' et 'avoir' ", 121). Our concept of transitivity is based on a purely formal criterion: the ability of a verb to take an accusative object.

ingly, *imeťsja* equals *imeť* + Intransitive Marker. Since, as we know, *imeťsja* in Russian is synonymous with existential *byť*, it follows that the relationshaip between existential *byť* and the verb *iméť* can be reduced to a single grammatical marker: *byť* is *iméť* minus transitivity. A similar construction is found in Czech. The Czech equivalent of English 'How *are* you?' is 'Jak *se máš/máte?*'. In other words, the reflexive verb *mít se* (literally 'to have oneself') in one of its usages is equivalent to *be*.

Thus Russian *iméť* and *byť* constructions can be said to represent two different grammatical solutions, or, if one wishes, two surface structures of one and the same underlying semantic structure which can be implemented either as a transitive or as an intransitive noun-verb-noun relation.

If N^1 is inanimate, the transitive construction takes the shape of *Nom* + *iméť* + *Acc* or *Locative* + *byť/imetsja* + *Nom*. Both constructions are admitted, if between the first and the second noun there exists a relation of 'spatial inclusion' (N^2 is spatially included in N^1). Such a relation exists in 'The house has two apartments', 'The apartment has a large bathroom', 'The room has two entrances', etc. The Russian equivalents are *V dóme (iméjutsja) dve kvartíry*, *V kvartíre iméetsja bořšája vánnaja*, *V kómnate (iméjutsja) dva vxóda*. Constructions with *iméť* are possible, though less 'idiomatic': *Dom iméet dve kvartíry*, *Kvartíra iméet boršúju vánnuju*, *Kómnata iméet dva vxóda*. But *iméť* constructions are impossible if there is no relation of 'spatial inclusion' between N^1 and N^2 as in

(32a) E The house has a garden.
   Germ Das Haus hat einen Garten.
   Cz Dům má záhradu, but
(32b) R *Dom iméet sad.

It is noteworthy that the Russian equivalents of sentences such as (32a) are implemented by *byť* constructions in which N^1 is used with the preposition *pri* semantically marked as 'adessive'.

(32c) *Pri* dóme (iméetsja) sad '*Next* to the house there is a garden'

The impossibility of using the construction *u* + *Gen* (**U doma esť/imeetsja sad*) shows that the Russian preposition *u* no longer has the adessive meaning, if it appears in *byť* constructions and in topic position [see sentences (4) to (6) in paragraph 3].

11. Logicians, semanticians and philosophers of language generally assume that there exists a 'logical' relation *A has B*, implicitly considering this relation to be 'universal'. But, as every linguist should know, 'have' *qua* lexeme is a rarity among the languages of the world; 'the majority of the languages do not know it'.[33] *A has B* is a linguistic construction typical for H-languages and is being gradually adopted by some B-languages. The assumption of a 'universal' *A has B* relation reflects egocentrical thinking of theoreticians biased by their linguistic background.[34]

Latin *Mihi erat amicus*, Hungarian *Nekem volt egy barátom* 'To me was one friend of mine', Russian *U menjá byl drug* 'With respect to me there was a friend' do not contain the slightest trace of a *have*-relation. The 'dative' constructions of Latin or Hungarian and the the *u + Gen* construction of Russian are different grammatical devices to signal implication or concern of a person with respect to the validity of a statement. There is not even a hint of 'possessivity' in Russian sentences like (32c).

An independent and self-contained sentence such as

(33) Syn účitsja v Moskvé 'The son studies in Moscow.'

may be expanded by an element establishing a specific relation of 'implication' between a speaker and the message conveyed by the sentence:

(33a) Syn *u menjá* účitsja v Moskvé.

A similar relation of implication is established in some H-languages by a *have*-construction, as in English *I have a son studying in Moscow*, or by a dative, as in Czech *Syn mi studuje v Moskvě*.[35]

---

[33] E. Benveniste, " 'Être' et 'avoir' ", 121.
[34] It is noteworthy, however, that even Apresjan, a native speaker of Russian, considers *imét* 'have' to be an 'elementary semantic feature', a semantic prime — *Èksperimental'noe issledovanie russkogo glagola* (Moscow, 1967), 9. M. Bierwisch posits a general *have*-relation (X has Y) for German, assuming that this relation includes the relation 'Y is part of X' — "Eine Hierarchie syntaktisch-semantischer Merkmale", *Studia Grammatica* V (Berlin, 1965), 29–86. The semantic elusiveness of the relation *A has B* is discussed (for German nouns denoting body parts) in A. V. Isačenko, "Das grammatische Verhalten der Bezeichnungen von Körperteilen im Deutschen", *Studia Grammatica* V (Berlin, 1965), 7–28.
[35] Cf. R. Mrázek and J. Brym, "Semantika a funkce ruského genitivu", 104.

The same relation of implication can be observed in the following examples, mostly taken from Mrázek and Brym:

(34) U bábuški bolít golová 'Grandma has a headache.'
(35) U bábuški ubežála kóška 'Grandma is implicated in the fact that the cat ran away.'
(36) U bábuški drožát rúki 'Grandma's hands are trembling.'
(37) U bábuški velosipéd v garažé 'Grandma has a/the bicycle in the garage.'
(38) U bábuški rodilás' vnúčka 'A granddaughter was born to grandma.'

Note that *bolít golová, ubežála kóška, velosipéd E v garažé* are well-formed and self-contained sentences which do not require any further specifications.

Similarly, *Esť dén'gi* 'There is money' is a well-formed and self-contained Russian sentence which does not require any further specification. The addition of the implicational prepositional phrase in *U menjá esť dén'gi* is nothing more than an adverbial expansion of the sentence *Esť dén'gi*. Only the existence of parallel *imét'* constructions creates the illusion that *U menjá esť dén'gi* is a special token of the *have*-relation in Russian. This brings us to the problem of 'possessivity' in general.

12. The Latin grammatical term *possessivus* was accepted into the grammatical terminology of all European languages; it refers to a class of pronouns, adjectives, adnominal genitive and dative constructions, predicative relations expressed by 'possessive' sentences. For all their inventiveness, contemporary linguists continue to be under the spell of conventional grammatical terms which they tend to hypostatize. The 'possessive relation' is believed to be a linguistic 'universal'. Otherwise Lyons could not have written that "in many, and perhaps in all, languages existential and possessive constructions derive ... from locatives".[36] Only in a very limited number of usages do 'possessives' really refer to what may be labelled 'possession'. Even *my house* is not necessarily the house which I possess; *my house* could be just as well the house I am living in, the house I particularly like, or the house I have in mind. In what meaningful sense can the sentence *We have fair weather today* be called possessive? What kind of 'possessivity' is expressed by *my*

[36] "A Note on Possessive, Existential and Locative Sentences", 390.

case, my body, my sister, my wife, my contemporary, my age, my impression, my statement, my tailor, my native town? An interesting attempt to distinguish, in Russian and Czech, possessive constructions proper and to delimit them from other constructions was undertaken by R. Zimek.[37]

Many languages use adnominal genitive and adnominal dative constructions which are called 'possessive'. Thus, in Old Church Slavic the adnominal dative in constructions of the type $N^1 + N^2/$dat is optional, if (a) N^1 is a personal noun and N^2 a personal noun referring to kinship, or (b) both nouns are non-personal.

Examples for (a): *bratъ mi* 'my brother', *synъ mi* 'my son', *otrokъ mi* 'my child', *blizokъ mi* 'my relative', etc.

Examples for (b): *solь zemli* (Dat) 'salt of the earth', *xramъ molitvě* 'house of prayer', *prazdьnikъ pascě* 'the feast of Easter', *vъ věky vekomъ* 'forever and ever' (lit. 'for ages of ages').[38]

The dative in (b) expresses relations which are clearly different from what is usually called 'possession'. Just as the adnominal genitive in Russian *probléma snabžénija* 'the problem of supply' evidently goes back to the predicative *be*-construction *Snabžénie E probléma* 'supply is a problem', the OCS construction *prazdьnikъ pascě* is a transformed *be*-construction *pasxa estъ prazdьnikъ*. Neither the 'surface structure', nor any kind of conceivable 'deep structure' contains so much as a hint of a 'possessive' relation. The same is true of the examples quoted under (a). Kinship relations have nothing to do with possession. Note that Russian uses special quasi-auxiliary verbs to denote this specific kind of kinship relation: *On mne prixóditsja (dovóditsja) dvojúrodnym brátom, šúrinom* 'He is my cousin, my brother-in-law'. There is really nothing in the semantics of such sentences which would justify calling constructions like *moj dvojúrodnyj brat* or OCS *bratrъ mi* 'my brother' 'possessive'.

Let us consider 'possession' in Hungarian, a typical B-language. What appears to be a 'possessive' suffix in Hungarian is in reality nothing but a personal marker which may be added to both nouns or verbs:

---

[37] R. Zimek, "K chápání posesivnosti", *Rusko-české studie, Sborník Vysoké školy pedagogické v Praze, Jazyk a literatura (Kopeckij-Festschrift)* II (1960), 131–156.

[38] Cf. J. Kurz, *Učebnice jazyka staroslověnského* (Prague, 1969), 208.

Personal markers in nouns		Personal markers in verbs	
kép-e-m	'my picture'	kér-e-m	'I ask'
kép-e-d	'thy picture'	kér-e-d	'thou ask'
kép-e-Ø	'his picture'	kér-i-Ø	'he asks'
kép-ünk	'our picture'	kér-j-ük	'we ask'
kép-e-tek	'your picture'	kér-i-tek	'you ask'
kép-ü-k	'their picture'	kér-i-k	'they ask'

There is no special 'possessive' pronoun in Hungarian. In its most explicit form the construction corresponding to *My book* is *Az én képem* where *az* is the article, *én* is 'I' and *képem*, the '1st person singular form' of the noun *kép*. The very general relation of 'implication' is expressed (redundantly) by two markers *(én, -em)*, but 'implication' is not 'possession'.

12.1 Possession proper or 'ownership' is a legal institution appearing in societies after they have reached a certain stage of development. It is instructive to compare the verbs related to ownership in H-languages with those in B-languages.

English *to own*, Germ *besitzen*, Czech *vlastnit* are transitive verbs belonging to the domestic stock of the vocabulary.[39] Russian, a typical B-language, has no domestic transitive verb meaning 'to own, to possess'. The verbs *vladéť* and *obladáť* used as equivalents of 'possess' mean primarily 'to be master of, to govern', derived from the stem *vlad-* 'reign'. Both words are borrowings from Slavonian. They govern the instrumental (and not the accusative) and have a variety of meanings which are not covered by MoE *own*, Germ *besitzen*, Cz *vlastnit*, e.g. *vladéť jazykóm* 'know (how to speak) a language' (loan-translation from Germ *eine Sprache beherrschen*), *vladéť sobój* 'to control oneself' (Germ *sich beherrschen*), *obladáť xorošim slúxom* 'to have a good ear'.

12.2 Constructions such as *A owns B* may be converted into synonymous constructions *B belongs to A*. The verbs *own* and *belong* may be called conversives. In H-languages the verbs meaning 'belong' are part of the fundamental domestic vocabulary: MoE *belong*,

---

[39] MoE *own* is related to Goth *áigan* 'to own', AS *āgan*, Germ *eigen*. Germ *besitzen* is an old loan-translation from Lat *possedere*. Polish has adopted Lat *possedere* to *posiadać* 'to own', Cz *vlastnit* 'own' is derived from *vlastní* 'own, proper (adj.)'.

Germ *gehören*, Cz *patřit*. But Russian *pri-nadležát'* is a late borrowing from Slavonian; it is not quoted in Sreznevskij *Materialy*, including the Dopolnenija.

In H-languages, the verbs meaning 'to belong' acquire a variety of secondary meanings not shared by R *prinadležát'*:

(39) He belongs to the family
    Germ Er gehört zur Familie
    Cz   Patří do rodiny

(39a) *On prinadležít k sem'é
    (correct: On E člen sem'í)

(40) She belongs in the theater
    Germ Sie gehört ans Theater
    Cz   Patř' do divadla

(40a) *Ona prinadležít v teátr
    (correct: Ej by v teátre byt')

(41) This belongs in another chapter
    Germ Das gehört in ein anderes Kapitel
    Cz   To patří do jiné kapitoly

(41a) *Èto prinadležít v drugúju glavú (∼ 'Èto sjudá ne otnósitsja').

It is clear that the relation of 'ownership' and its conversive, the only relation which deserves the name 'possessive', has different implementations in *have* and *be* languages. We should be more careful in positing linguistic 'universals' and making far reaching generalizations on the basis of a few trivial examples. Those who are so concerned about linguistic 'universals', i.e. structural features valid in ALL languages of the world, should remember that it is useful to know at least some of them.

13. *Be* constructions belong to the most elementary syntactic patterns of IE languages. Sentences of the type *A is B* cannot be further reduced or simplified. Semantically the verb *be* is the most abstract verb with a large variety of different connotations and functions. Both *A* and *B* in *be* constructions may be implemented by a variety of word classes having a number of different grammatical markers.

In some languages *have* has become a verb nearly as elementary as *be*. It has entered various semantic and syntactical relations with *be* and has eventually become embedded in an intricate network of semantic and syntactical correlations with other verbs which doubtlessly belong to the elementary (abstract) verbs of the language. These facts justify in our view the term '*have* languages'.

As has been shown in (5), *imét'* constructions in Russian first appear in bookish styles and penetrate into the spoken language not before the 19th century. As we have seen, *imét'* entered into a number of syntactical and semantic correlations with different usages of the verb *byt'*, but characteristically was not embedded in significant semantic and syntactical correlations with other 'elementary' verbs. This justifies, in our view, our assumption that Russian, although having adopted a number of *imét'* constructions, remains up to this day a typical B-language. Let us consider the pertinent facts.

13.1. There exists in H-languages a very intimate relation between the verbs *have* and *get*. In English, constructions with the present of *have* are synonymous with constructions using the perfect of *get*: *I have some money/I've got some money*. The original meaning of *get* 'to obtain' is effaced in *I've got plenty of time (*I have obtained plenty of time)*.

In H-languges, verbs meaning 'get, obtain' tend to become correlated with *have* in a very specific manner: 'get, obtain' is interpreted as an inchoative of *have*, meaning 'begin to have'.

In Russian the verb *polučít'/polučát'* 'to obtain' has no structural similarities with either *imét'* or *byt'*. It is clearly correlated with 'addressive' verbs such as *dat'* 'give', *podarít'* 'give as a gift', *poslát'* 'send', *otprávit'* 'id.', *vručít'* 'hand over, present', etc., all of them being combined with a 'dative of the addressee'. In other words, R *Ja polučíl ot negó désjat' rubléj* 'I got ten roubles from him' refers to the same situation as *On dal (poslál, vručíl) mne désjat rubléj* 'He gave (sent, handed over to) me ten roubles'. This semantic correlation prevails, of course, in English as well. But R *polučít'* never is used in constructions where there is no 'donor', cf.

(42a) I have an idea   I got an idea 'I began to have an idea'
(42b) We have a new teacher   We got a new teacher 'began to have'

Constructions corresponding to (42) are quite normal in other H-languages, such as German or Czech:

(42c) G   Ich habe eine Idee   Ich bekam eine Idee
      Cz   Mám nápad   Dostal jsem nápad

(42d)
G Wir haben einen neuen Lehrer   Wir bekamen einen neuen Lehrer
Cz Máme nového učitele   Dostali jsme nového učitele.

But in Russian it is impossible to say *Ja polučil idéju, *My polučili novogo učitelja. In fact, the bundle of semantic features 'begin' + 'have' does not exist in Russian. The Russian equivalents of (42b) would be *U nas tepér' nóvyj učitel'.*[40]

13.2. German *bekommen*, Czech *dostat* 'get' are used as inchoatives of *have* with abstract nouns in object position, the presence of a 'donor' being excluded:

(43a) Germ Ich habe Angst   Ich bekam Angst 'I got scared'
      Cz   Mám strach   Dostal jsem strach
(43b) Germ Ich habe Hunger   Ich bekam Hunger 'got hungry'
      Cz   Mám hlad   Dostal jsem hlad

In Russian, where there is no *Ja iméju strax, *Ja iméju gólod, there is also no *Ja polučil strax, *Ja polučil golod. The inchoative of the Russian *be* construction *Mne E strášno* 'I am scared' is implemented by the verb *stat'/stanovit'sja* which is correlated with *byt'* and means 'begin to be':

(43c) Mne E strašno Mne *stálo* strášno 'To me it began to be fearful'

It is noteworthy that English *get* fulfils a double function: it is used as an inchoative of *have* (*I got a cold* 'began to have') and as an inchoative of *be* (*I am scared/I got scared* 'began to be'). Diachronically, the semantic affinity between the inchoatives of *be* and *have* is documented by the fact that Germanic *bi-queman* originally meant 'come to be' (as in MoE *become a man*), but was reinterpreted in German as 'come to have' (as in Germ *einen Brief bekommen*).

13.3. In H-languages the verb *give* is, in one of its usages, closely related to the verb *have*. In fact, *give* in H-languages is the causative of *have*: English *It gives me a headache* may be analyzed as 'it causes me to have a headache'. H-languages use *give*-constructions for which there are no direct equivalents in B-languages, cf.

[40] The idiomatic equivalent of (42c) in Russian would be *Mne prišlá v gólovu idéja* lit. 'An idea came to my head'.

(44a) Cz Mám s tým hodně práce 'I have a lot of work with this.'
(44b) To mi dá hodně práce 'This gives me a lot of work (causes me to have).'

In Russian analogical *give*-constructions are unthinkable, cf. *Èto mne daët mnógo vozní, since *byt́* in the underlying construction *U menjá s ètim E mnógo vozní* is not correlated with *dat́/davát́*.

There exist in Russian numerous more or less idiomatic constructions in which *imét́* and *dat́* are correlated: *imét́/dat́ právo* 'have/give the right', *imét́/dat́ slóvo* 'have/give the floor', etc. But there is no correlation between *u* + *Gen* + *byt́* and *dat́/davát́* in Russian.

13.4. In H-languages the verbs *get* and *give* can be analyzed as different modifications of *have* ('begin to have' vs. 'cause to have'). This makes *get* and *give* conversives in H-languages, cf. *I got a shot/ They gave me a shot*. This semantic correlation of *get* and *give* is typical for H-languages:

45a) Germ   Ich bekam eine Injektion   'I got a shot'
     Cz   Dostal jsem injekci
(45b) Germ Man gab mir eine Injektion   'They gave me a shot'
     Cz   Dali mi injekci

The absence of the verb *have* in the central sphere of Russian syntax precludes the possibility of correlating *get* and *give* unless the object is a physical one. This is why we do not find either **Ja polučíl ukól* 'I got a shot', or **Mne dáli ukól* 'They gave me a shot' in Russian. The causative construction uses the verb *sdélat́* 'to make' which can be analyzed into 'cause to be' as in *Egó sdélali sekretarëm* 'They made him (caused him to be) a secretary'. Accordingly, the Russian equivalent of (45b) is

(45c) *Mne sdélali ukól* 'They made me a shot'.

The semantic relation between *sdélat́* and *byt́* becomes manifest if the verb appears with the intransitive marker -*sja*. Transitive *sdélat́* + *sja* mean 'to become' = 'to begin to be' as in *On sdélalsja sekretarëm* 'He became a secretary'. Thus *sdélat́sja* is synonymous with *stat́*, see sentence (43c). The inchoatives *sdelát́sja* and *stat́* (and their imperfective equivalents) are correlated with *u* + *Gen* + *byt́* constructions; in H-languages we find in comparable sentences the correlation between 'get' and 'have':

(46a) Germ Er hat einen Anfall   (46b) R U negó E pripádok
     Cz   Má záchvat   'He is having an attack'
(47a) Germ Er bekam einen Anfall (47b) R S nim sdélalsja pripádok
     Cz   Dostal záchvat   'He got an attack'

13.4. In the majority of *get* and *give* constructions, Czech and Slovak, as a rule, follow German. But having become typical H-languages, Czech and Slovak have developed *give* constructions unparallelled in other H-languages.

When studying the menu in a restaurant, a husband may ask his wife 'What shall we have?'. The equivalent question in Czech uses *give*:

(48)   Cz Co si dáme? 'What shall we give to ourselves?'

Since *dát* 'give' in Czech is equivalent to 'cause to have', the following sentences are almost synonymous:

(49)   Dali jsme si guláš a pivo 'We had ourselves goulash and a beer.'

(50)   Měli jsme guláš a pivo 'We had goulash and a beer.'

Note that 'have' in (50) has nothing to do with 'possession'.

The Russian equivalent of (49) is a $u + Gen + byt'$ construction:

(49a)   R U nas byl guljáš i pívo.

Constructions parallel to Czech (49) (*My sebe dali . . .) are unthinkable in Russian.

14.1. The verb *have* may be used with reference to the opposite of 'possession'. When complaining about high living costs, a Czech housewife may say: 'You buy some butter, eggs, meat and fruits and right away *you have* a hundred (crowns)':

(51)   Koupíš máslo, vejce, maso a ovoce a hned *máš* stovku.

Accumulating spendings is not accumulating 'possessions', and yet a H-language uses the verb *have*. Far from even hinting at anything like 'possession', *have*-constructions boil down to *be*-constructions with the person implicated standing as the subject of the sentence.

15. In H-languages the verb *have* has the tendency to become 'grammaticalized', i.e. to serve as a modal modifier of other verbs. There are numerous instances of this development.

15.1. H-languages use the verb *have* in negative sentences with pronouns (or pronominal adverbs) and the infinitive. In analogical constructions Russian uses the verb *be*:

(52) He *had* nothing to say (52a) R Emú néčego *bylo* skazát
 Cz Ne*měl* co říci
(53) He *had* nobody to consult (53a) Emú né s kem *bylo* posovétovatsja
 Cz Ne*měl* se s kým poradit
(54) He *had* nowhere to go (54a) Emú nékuda *bylo* idtí
 Cz Ne*měl* kam jít

In this sentence pattern there is a one-to-one correspondence between *have* in H-languages and 'be' in Russian.

15.2. H-languages use the verb *have* + Infinitive to express necessity:

(55a) You have to answer (55b) Germ Du hast zu antworten
(55c) Cz Máš odpovídat (55d) Slk Máš odpovedať

The modality expressed by this construction differs slightly from language to language. In English it may be equivalent to 'must', in German it may express in some contexts 'inevitable future'. In French we find the construction *ne* + *avoir* + *que* + *infinitive* meaning 'need':

(55e) Il n'a qu'à répondre 'He has only to answer'.

In Czech and Slovak the verbs *míti/mať* 'have' correspond to German *sollen*: Cz *Nemáš kouřit*, Slk *Nemáš fajčiť*, Germ *Du sollst nicht rauchen* mean 'You should not smoke'.

Czech and Slovak share with German the usage of *have* + *infinitive* to signal a 'reported event':

(56a) Germ Der Verfasser *soll* ein Mönch gewesen sein
 'The author is said to have been a monk'
(56b) Cz Autorem *měl* být mních.

Russian constructions with *imét'* + Infinitive with the meaning of 'certain future' are rare, obsolete and have a distinctly clerical flavor: *Soobščénie iméet pojavít'sja v gazétax* 'The information is to appear in the papers'. Constructions of this type are restricted to a few verbs only. Neither in good fiction nor in colloquial Russian would one find *iméť* in combination with verbs such as *kupíť* 'to buy', *výkupaťsja* 'to take a bath', or *umeréť* 'to die' (cf. *On iméet umeréť 'He is to die').

Modal verbs belong to the innermost layer of the vocabulary of a language. H-languages have incorporated the verb *have* into their system of modal verbs. In Russian the constructions with *iméť* + Infinitive are an 'altogether foreign element'.[41] They are loan-translations from German and have not been internalized in the language.

15.3. In H-languages constructions with *have* + Infinitive may lose their modal character and become grammatical markers of the future. This happened in the majority of Romance languages, where Low Latin *cantare habeo* yielded, as in French, the future form *je chanterai*. A similar process took place in East Slavic.

In East Slavic we find from the 11th to the 16th century two constructions corresponding to Low Latin *cantare habeo*:

(a) *imamь/iměju* + Infinitive (perfective or imperfective);
(b) *imu* + Infinitive (only imperfective).

It seems almost incredible that not a single Russian or Ukrainian investigator ever noticed that these two constructions had very distinct functions and referred to quite different situations.[42] Furthermore, the two constructions belong to two different linguistic layers. It is the great merit of the young Czech linguist Helena Křížková to have given the first adequate and exhaustive analysis of these constructions in East Slavic.[43]

---

[41] 'polnostju prišlyj èlement', S. P. Obnorskij, *Očerki po morfologii russkogo glagola* (Moscow, 1953), 161.
[42] Cf. I. I. Sreznevskij, *Materialy dlja slovarja drevnerusskogo jazyka* I (St. Petersburg, 1893), s.v. *iměti*. — P. Lavrovskij, *O jazyke severnyx russkix letopisej* (St. Petersburg, 1852), 89. — F. I. Buslaev, *Istoričeskaja grammatika russkogo jazyka* (Moscow, 1881), 211-212. — A. I. Sobolevskij, *Lekcii po istorii russkogo jazyka* (4th ed.; Moscow, 1907), 237. — A. Kryms'kyj, *Narysy z istoriï ukraïns'koï movy* (Kiev, 1922), 104. — N. Durnovo, *Očerk istorii russkogo jazyka* (Moscow, 1924), 235. — L. P. Jakubinskij, *Istorija drevnerusskogo jazyka* (Moscow, 1953), 237-238. — T. P. Lomtev, *Očerki po istoričeskomu sintaksisu russkogo jazyka* (Moscow, 1956), 65. — V. I. Borkovskij and P. S. Kuznecov, *Istoričeskaja grammatika russkogo jazyka* (Moscow, 1963), 261-262.
[43] Helena Křížková, "Vývoj opisného futura v jazycích slovanských, zvláště v ruštině", *Acta Universitatis Palackianae Olomucensis, Facultas Philosophica* 4, *L, Philologica* II (Prague, 1960).

According to H. Křížková, construction (a) originally had various modal meanings ranging from necessity to inevitability, where it becomes difficult to distinguish it from genuine future. Construction (a) occurs exclusively in Slavonian texts, including the Chronicles, and is totally unknown to the vernacular in the northeast of the East Slavic territory. Being a Slavonism, *imamь* + Infinitive usually renders Greek constructions with ἔχειν 'have',[44] but occasionally translates other Greek constructions as well.

Legal documents of the northeastern ('Great Russian') area never use constructions of the type (a), but in documents written on the territory of present-day Ukraine and Belorussia, constructions with *iměju/imaju/maju* + Infinitive are not infrequent,[45] showing the progressive proliferation of *have* in Ukrainian and Belorussian. In these texts the constructions have still a modal meaning: *majutь davaty* 'they should give' (1593).[46]

In contradistinction to (a), the constructions with *imu* + Infinitive have originally the 'phasal' meaning 'to begin to', similarly as the constructions with *na-, u-, po-čnú* + Inf. Constructions of the type (b) do not occur in Slavonian texts; their domain is the legal documents which reflect the vernacular.[47] They also occur in those passages of the Chronicles which reflect the spoken language, e.g. *pogani imutь radovati sja* 'the pagans will begin to rejoice' in the Primary Chronicle. During the 16th century *imu* + Inf. constructions begin to become rare until they are replaced by constructions with *stánu* and eventually by *budu* + Inf. *Imu* + Inf. still survives in northern Russian dialects (Novgorod, Kostroma, Jaroslavľ, Vologda, etc.), but the actual meaning of this periphrastic form remains unclear.[48]

On the other hand, constructions of the type (b) survived in Ukrainian and partly in the Belorussian area. According to Ukrai-

---

[44] See H. Birnbaum, "Zum analytischen Ausdruck der Zukunft im Altkirchenslavischen", *ZfslPh* 25 (1956), 1–7; H. Birnbaum, "Zum periphrastischen Futurum im Gotischen und Altkirchenslavischen", *Byzantinoslavica* 18 (1957), 77–81. H. Birnbaum, *Untersuchungen zu den Zukunftsumschreibungen mit dem Infinitiv im Altkirchenslavischen: Ein Beitrag zur historischen Verbalsyntax des Slavischen* (Stockholm, 1958), 61–129 and 213–220.
[45] H. Křížková, "Vývoj opisného futura", 118–119.
[46] *Ibid.*, 119.
[47] *Ibid.*, 127.
[48] *Ibid.*, 136. See also G. Wytrzens, "Zur Frage des periphrastischen Futurums im Russischen", *Wiener slavistisches Jahrbuch* III (1953), 21 ff.

nian grammarians, *robytymu* (= *robyty* + *imu*) does not differ semantically from *budu robyty* 'I shall work'. The contracted forms do not appear before the first half of the 15th century.[49]

Under the influence of Polish, which very early begins to incorporate *have*-constructions, Ukrainian and Belorussian are becoming H-languages. The close genetic relationship between Ukrainian and Belorussian, on the one hand, and Russian, on the other, did not prevent the former from becoming typologically very different from the latter.

15.4. H-languages regularly develop periphrastic past tenses in which *have* functions as an 'auxiliary'. The replacement in Latin of *mihi est aliquid* by *habeo aliquam rem* permitted the introduction of constructions like *habeo opus factum* 'I have the work done'. In Romance languages *habeo* + past participle yielded a paradigmatic form, cf. French *j'ai fait* 'I have done'.[50] According to Benveniste, the transitive perfect in Germanic is an autonomous development which is independent from Latin.[51] It exists in Gothic and Old Icelandic and is reflected by MoE *I have forgotten*, Germ *Ich habe vergessen*.[52]

This development is repeated in such Slavic H-languages as Czech and Slovak. There exist in both languages very productive constructions consisting of *have* + accusative noun + perfective past participle. This pattern is rapidly spreading in the colloquial varieties; in Slovak they are already considered 'literary', in Czech they still seem to be substandard:

(57) Slk Mám polievku uvarenú 'I have the soup cooked'.
(58) Mám peniaze odložené 'I have the money put aside'.
(59) Máš to tu napísané 'You have it written here'.

Pauliny considers these forms ('stative perfect') to belong to the

---

[49] H. Křížková, "Vývoj opisného futura", 131.
[50] Reflexive verbs as well as certain verbs of motion form the periphrastic perfect by means of the auxiliary *être* 'be', e.g. *je me suis fait, je suis allé*.
[51] E. Benveniste, " 'Être' et 'avoir' ", 134.
[52] In German, the periphrastic perfect is formed with the auxiliary *sein* 'be', if the verb is intransitive and has the general meaning of a 'directional process' ('gerichteter Vorgang'), e.g. *ich bin gekommen, gegangen, gefahren, ich bin aufgestanden, eingeschlafen, aufgewacht*, etc. Cf. W. Steinitz, "Die Erforschung der deutschen Sprache der Gegenwart", *Wissenschaftliche Annalen* I, 8 (Berlin: Akademie-Verlag, November 1952), 496.

paradigm of the perfective Slovak verb,⁵³ but the newest edition of the Slovak Academy Grammar does not consider them to be special temporal forms.⁵⁴ The sentences quoted are semantically distinct from the preterite constructions: *Uvaril som polievku, Odložil som peniaze* in very much the same way, as English 'I have the soup cooked' differs from 'I have cooked the soup'.⁵⁵

In Russian there are, of course, no comparable *imét'* constructions *(*Ja iméju sup svárennyj)*, but the perfective past (passive) participle is embedded into a *u + Gen + byt* construction:

(57a) U menjá sup E sváren.
(58a) U menjá dén'gi E otlóženy.

In Russian dialects we find constructions such as *U menjá E xóženo* 'I have walked (much)' where the 'impersonal' form is used and the verb is intransitive and imperfective.

One of the main characteristics of B-languages is the fact that they do not make use of the 'auxiliary' verb *have*.

16. The proliferation of *have* constructions in a language seems to trigger substantial changes in the system of other auxiliaries. Along with *be* and *have*, English has not only preserved the Germanic preterite-presents *can, may, must*, but developed some new modal auxiliaries such as *ought to* and *need*. German uses the modal auxiliaries *können, mögen, dürfen, müssen, sollen*. In French where *être* and *avoir* are the central auxiliaries, we find the verbs *devoir* 'must', *pouvoir* 'can', *savoir* 'know, be able to' and the verbs *faire* 'make' and *laisser* 'let' which behave very much like auxiliaries. Certain modal relations are expressed by constructions with *avoir*, e.g. French *j'ai besoin* 'I need'.

Russian, on the other hand, inherited from Common Slavic the modal verbs *mogú* 'I can' and *xočú* 'I want to'. All other modal relations are expressed either by adjectival *be* constructions (*Ja E dólžen* 'I must'), or by dative constructions with special indeclinables called predicatives (of nominal origin): *Mne E nádo* 'I need', *Mne E núžno* 'id.', *Mne E móžno* 'I may', *Mne E nel'zjá* 'I may not',

---

⁵³ E. Pauliny, *Slovenské časovanie* (Bratislava, 1949), 55.
⁵⁴ Cf. J. Ružička, ed., *Morfológia slovenského jazyka* (Bratislava, 1966), 501.
⁵⁵ Cf. the sentence *I have the work done* as opposed to *I have done the work*, or the ambiguous sentence *I had a book stolen*, quoted by N. Chomsky, *Aspects of the Theory of Syntax* (Cambridge: M. I. T. Press, 1965), 22.

Mne E dólžno 'I must', etc.⁵⁶ Analogical *be*-constructions occur also in Hungarian, another typical B-language: *nekem lehet E* 'to me possible (is)', *nekem szabad E* 'to me permitted (is)'. Even the form *muszáj* borrowed from German *müssen* (or rather *er muβ* 'he must') is not a verb, but a modal predicative used in dative *be*-constructions: *nekem muszáj E* 'to me (it is a) must'.

Could it be sheer coincidence that those Slavic languages which have become H-languages since the Middle Ages (Czech, Slovak, Serbo-Croatian) and those which are on the verge of becoming H-languages (Polish, Ukrainian, Belorussian) have some modal verbs which are unknown to Russian, a B-language? German *muβ* 'must' was borrowed into Czech *(musím)*, Slovak *(musím)*, Polish *(muszę)* and penetrated through Polish into Ukrainian *(mušu)* and Belorussian *(musić)*. Upper Sorbian has the modal verb *dyrbjeć* 'to have to' borrowed from OHG *durfan* (Germ *dürfen*) and attested also in Old Czech. Czech and Slovak have transformed the Common Slavic verb **směti* 'to dare' into a modal auxiliary Cz *smím*, Slk *smiem* 'I may'. In Serbo-Croatian we find not only *mòci/mògu* 'I can', but also *mórati/môrām* 'I must', etc. What is more, nominal modal expressions (case forms of nouns, prepositional phrases) tend to become modal verbs in Slavic H-languages. Thus Czech *lze* and *nelze* (originally a Loc. sing. of the noun *lьza*) add in the past tense the verbal past neuter singular marker *-lo* in *lzelo* and *nelzelo*; these forms are no longer considered standard, but they still occurred in 20th century clerical Czech and are widespread in substandard and dialects. The predicative expression *treba* (originally a Nom. sing. fem. noun) used in the present without a present *be* form in Slovak takes the verbal marker *-lo* in the past tense: *trebalo*, a form which is known to many dialects. In Serbo-Croatian the noun **trěba* 'sacrifice' was interpreted as an 'impersonal' verb with the 3rd person sing. form *treba* 'it is necessary' and the perfect *trebalo je* 'it was necessary'. In colloquial speech the original construction *treba mi knjiga* is changed into *ja trebam knjigu* 'I need a book' and thus

---

⁵⁶ Cf. A. V. Isačenko, *Grammatičeskij stroj russkogo jazyka v sopostavlenii s slovackim* (2nd ed.; Bratislava, 1965), 278–292. — A. V. Isačenko, "O vozniknovenii i razvitii 'kategorii sostojanija' v slavjanskix jazykax", *Voprosy jazykoznanija* 6, 1955, 48–65. See also H. Birnbaum, *Studies on Predication in Russian*, I. *Predicative Case, Short Form Adjectives and Predicatives*, (Memorandum RM-3774-PR, Santa Monica: The Rand Corporation, January 1964).

secondary transitivity was attached to the modal expression (cf. R *mne núžno knígu* 'I need a book').

The attitude of Bulgarian and Macedonian towards the *have/be* dichotomy has not been treated here, since the pertinent facts can be best treated in a wider framework of Balkan areal linguistics.

17. In the preceding paragraphs we have tried to show the profound structural differences existing between languages in which '*have*' as a lexeme has been fully internalized and those languages in which this lexeme either does not exist at all, or is restricted only to certain layers of the more bookish syntax. In languages of the first type, the verb *have* enters into various syntactic and semantic relations with such fundamental verbs as *get* or *give* and is utilized in a variety of constructions which cannot be simply identified as 'possessive'. Furthermore, in these languages *have* penetrates into the grammatical system and becomes a formal marker of tense forms and of different modalities. In languages such as Russian, the late penetration of *have* did not have any noticeable effect on the overall semantic structure and did not affect the morphology of the verb.

In one of his brilliant papers on metalinguistic problems, B. L. Whorf has demonstrated that the typically Western (or 'mechanical') approach to reality was due to a great extent to the Western Indo-European syntactic sentence pattern consisting of Actor + Action+Goal, which he called Standard Average European, with the 'possible (but doubtful) exception of Balto-Slavic'.[57] Whorf pointed out that "English pattern treats 'I hold it' exactly like 'I strike it', 'I tear it' .... Yet 'hold' in plain fact is no action, but a state of relative positions".[58] We know that the lexeme *have* developed in IE from verbs meaning 'hold', 'grasp' (2); the meaning of *have* is more abstract than that of 'hold'; *have* no longer expresses a state of relative positions in space, in fact, its general meaning can be analyzed as *be* + Transitivity (10.1). The lexeme *have* was made to fit into the overall Western Indo-European pattern of transitive constructions of the type *A Xes B*.

One of the purposes of our investigation was to show that 'Balto-

---

[57] B. L. Whorf, *Language, Thought and Reality* (Cambridge: M. I. T. Press, 1956), 138.
[58] *Ibid.*, p. 262.

Slavic' by no means represents a uniform group of languages with respect to the usage of *have* and *be* constructions. Within Baltic, Lithuanian became a H-language, while Latvian remained a B-language. Within Slavic, only Russian preserved its status as a typical B-language in spite of the fact that it introduced (at a late date) more or less bookish *have* constructions. On the other hand, Czech and Slovak became typical H-languages, pushing *have* constructions even farther than the Romance and Germanic languages. Thus, in Czech, one uses *have* constructions with prepositional phrases, e.g. *Mám po zkoušce*, literally 'I have after the examination' equivalent to German *Ich habe die Prüfung hinter mir* 'I have the examination behind me'. Thus Czech and Slovak, and, to a large extent Serbo-Croatian, Polish and Ukrainian belong clearly to the "Western" syntactic type, while Russian remains archaic (in more than one respect) and is only superficially affected by Western syntax.

It has been stressed that *have* as a lexeme is extremely rare among the languages of the world. The relations *A has B* is limited only to a few H-languages. Semanticians, logicians and philosophers of language should try to liberate themselves from their linguistic 'egocentrism' and cease to assume that whatever occurs in Western European syntax must be *eo ipso* 'universal'. The 'Gesamtbedeutung' of *have* is too abstract to justify its identification with 'possession'. It seems advisable not to operate with terms such as 'possession' or 'possessive' in general semantics, because such terms, not having any linguistically based correlates, obscure more than they reveal.

University of California, Los Angeles

A PROBLEM IN THE ANALYSIS OF SOME
$VOWEL \sim ZERO$ ALTERNATIONS IN MODERN RUSSIAN

THEODORE M. LIGHTNER

I assume that the underlying representations of the roots in forms like PES (gen. PSA) and MOX (gen. either MXA or MOXA) contain the lax vowels $ĭ$ and $ŭ$: $pĭs$ and $mŭx$, resp.[1] In §§ 1–3 a set of rules is given to govern the dropping and lowering of these lax, high vowels; the problem which this paper poses (§§ 4–5) concerns the formulation of a rule to govern the dropping and lowering of lax, high vowels in prefixes (OTO- $\sim$ OT- from $otŭ$-, and so on).

A few examples of underlying representations and the representations which must be derived from them are given below:

orthographic	underlying representation	derived representation
nom. sg. PES	$pĭs+ŭ$	$pés$[2]
gen. sg. PSA	$pĭs+á$	$psá$
nom. sg. PESIK	$pĭs+ĭk+ŭ$	$pésĭk$
gen. sg. PESIKA	$pĭs+ĭk+a$	$pésĭka$
n. s. (PERE-)ŠEJEK	$šéj+ŭk+ŭ$	$šéjok$
g. s. -ŠEJKA	$šéj+ŭk+a$	$šéjka$
n. s. -ŠEJEČEK	$šéj+uč+ĭk+ŭ$[3]	$šéjoček$

[1] The analyses proposed here are purely synchronic, although the underlying representations obviously reflect earlier historical stages of Russian; discussion, see Lightner (1966). The observation that underlying representations are particularly resistant to change and that the rules which derive phonetic representations reflect historical sound changes is by no means a new one (cf. *op. cit.*, p. 24 fn. 39).

[2] To derive the phonetic representation [pʲos], a rule of consonant palatalization and a rule backing e to o must be applied. I shall not be concerned with these rules in this paper; discussion, see Lightner (1969).

[3] The suffix represented here as $uč$ is, of course, the same suffix represented as uk in -ŠÉJEK, -ŠÉJKA. A rule which derives palatals from underlying velars before front vowels is responsible for this shift of uk to $uč$; discussion, see Lightner (1969).

g. s. -ŠEJEČKA	šéj+uč+ik+a	šéjočka
3 sg. pres ŽDET[4]	žid+é+t	ždét
3 sg. pres. BERET	bir+é+t	berét

§1. ANALYSIS I

Disregarding, for the moment, the problem of stress shift ($pis+ú \to pis+u$ etc.), we can propose the following three rules:[5]

*(LOWER)$_1$ {ú, í} → {ó, é}
*(LOWER)$_2$ {u, i} → {o, e} / ____C{u, i}, where C represents any number of non-vowels
*(DROP) {u, i} → Ø, where Ø represents "zero"

A few derivations:

	PESIKA	-ŠEJEČEK
und. repr:	pís+ĭk+a	šéj+uč+ik+u
*(LOWER)$_1$:	é	
*(LOWER)$_2$:		o e
*(DROP):		Ø
derived repr:	pésĭka	šéjoček

There are other VOWEL ~ ZERO alternations which suggest the possibility of proposing a general (= language-independent) constraint that STRESSED VOWELS MAY NOT BE DROPPED. Thus one finds stressed ĭ alternating with zero in infinitives (VEZTÍ but LÉZT') and stressed ĭ alternating with zero in imperatives (GOVORÍ but GOTÓV'). Again, one finds the root vowel in MOX dropped

---

[4] Note that the root in this form must contain a vowel in order to account for the root vowel which appears phonetically in clearly related forms like OŽIDAT'. Cf. also fn. 8 below.

[5] An asterisk is prefixed to the rules given below to indicate that these rules are not yet correctly formulated; a revised version of the rules is presented in §2 below.

There are a number of forms which lie outside the application of these rules and which I shall not treat here: LOB (gen. LBA) but LOBASTYJ for expected *LBASTYJ; IGRA (gen. pl. IGR) but IGORKA for expected *IGRKA; SLUŽBA (cf. SLUŽEBNYJ), but gen. pl. SLUŽB for expected *SLUŽEB, and so on.

when unstressed (gen. MXÁ) but retained when stressed (MÓXA).[6] Adopting the convention that stressed vowels may not be dropped permits the formulation of a word-final i-dropping rule with no mention of stress: IN IMPERATIVES AND INFINITIVES WORD-FINAL i DROPS (another restriction regarding consonant clusters is necessary to account for forms like PRÝGNI, but this has nothing to do with stress). The proposed convention will automatically block the application of this rule to forms like VEZTÍ and GOVORÍ.

§2. ANALYSIS II

Given the above three rules governing u and i, we see that the convention proposed for stressed vowels plays no role in the derivation of the synonymous genitive singular forms MXÁ ~ MÓXA: the rule which lowers stressed $ú$, $í$ ensures that underlying $múx+a$ will be realized as $móx+a$, regardless of whether one adopts the proposed convention or not. In order to make full use of this convention, therefore, let us revise the rules so that the dropping of u, i takes place before the lowering of u, i; this ordering will permit us to dispense altogether with the rule that lowers stressed $ú$, $í$:

(DROP)   {u, i} → ∅ except / ____ C{u, i}
(LOWER)   {u, i} → {o, e}

The derivation of the two genitive forms of MOX is now as follows:

underlying representation:	$múx+a$	$mux+á$
(DROP):	——	∅
(LOWER):	ó	——
derived representation:	$móxa$	$mxá$

If we consider now the two nominative forms of MOX (i.e., $mux+ú$ and $múx+u$), it is obvious that under the present analysis

---

[6] The two declensions of MOX could, of course, be handled by assuming the roots mux with end-stress and mox with root-stress. But such an analysis requires two underlying distinctions between the roots (difference in vowel quality and difference in stress pattern), whereas the analysis proposed below requires only one distinction between the roots (difference in stress pattern).

the end-stress form will result in *moxó rather than the correct móx. We must, therefore, include a stress-retraction rule to derive múx+u from mux+ú. Professor Isačenko has called my attention to the fact that a similar phenomenon occurs in imperatives of verbs like PIT', ŠIT', BIT', etc. These verbs (except for BRIT') all have end-stress throughout the present: P'JÚ, P'JĚŠ', P'JĚT, etc. But in the imperative, the root is stressed (PÉJ). The present tense forms are regular (thus pij+é+t results correctly in pjét, phonetically [p'jót] — cf. fn. 2 above). But verbs with end-stress throughout the present normally have end-stress in the imperative (VEDÚ, VEDĚŠ', VEDĚT, ... VEDÍ; KLADÚ, KLADĚŠ', KLADĚT, ... KLADÍ, etc.). One expects, therefore, to find end-stressed pij+í as the underlying representation of imperative PÉJ; the representation pij+í, however, results in *pjí (phonetically *[p'jí]). As mentioned above, ALL the PIT'-type verbs have imperative in -ÉJ rather than in *-JÍ. It seems necessary, then, to include in the grammar a stress-retraction rule to account for such end-stressed forms. Throughout the rest of this paper, I assume the application of such a rule to derive forms like múx+u from mux+ú and pij+í from pij+í.[7] More discussion, see Lightner (1972), pp. 390 ff.

§3. THE TREATMENT OF VERBS LIKE BRAT', ZVAT'

Comparison of the relatively few verbs like BRAT' (3 sg. BERĚT, root bir), ZVAT' (3 sg. ZOVĚT, root zuv) with verbs like ŽDAT' (3 sg. ŽDĚT, root žid), LGAT' (3 sg. LŽĚT, root lug)[8] reveals that the present tense forms of one set of verbs must be considered exceptional regardless of how one handles the vowels u, i. Under the analysis proposed in § 2 above, the verbs with underlying u, i lowered to e, o (BERĚT, ŽIVĚT, etc.) are the irregular ones:

underlying representation:	žid+é+t	bir+é+t
(DROP):	∅	∅
(LOWER):	——	——
derived representation:	ždét	*brét

---

[7] See Coats (1970a) for a detailed discussion of this rule.

[8] The root here must contain the high, lax vowel u in order to account for the root vowel which appears phonetically in clearly related forms like inf. OBLYGAT', nom. sg. LOŽ' (cf. gen. LŽI with the expected absence of the root vowel), and so on.

These forms will be handled by idiosyncratically specifying roots like *bir, zuv, dir* as −(DROP) in present tense forms. Regular roots like *žid, žir, ruv, tuk* will redundantly be marked +(DROP).[9] I am indebted to Professor Taranovsky for bringing to my attention the fact that the taboo verb SRAT' has alternant present tense forms (SRËT ∼ SERËT); those speakers who have only SERËT use the irregular (= specified −DROP) root *sir;* those speakers who have only SRËT use the regular (= specified +DROP) root *sir;* and those speakers who have SRËT ∼ SERËT in free variation use the root *sir* optionally specified either +DROP or −DROP. Professor Isačenko has observed that taboo forms often display such variation; compare, for example, the well-known doublet ÉT' ∼ ETÍ.[10]

Returning now to ŽDËT and BERËT, we have the following derivations:

underlying representations:	$žid+é+t$	$bir+é+t$
	+DROP	−DROP
(DROP):	∅	—
(LOWER):	—	e
derived representations:	ždét	berét

Henceforth, the feature specification +DROP will be suppressed in order to lighten the reader's task in following the derivations.

---

[9] See Lightner (1972) for a formal procedure to mark exceptions to a rule *n* as −RULE *n* and to mark the regular forms +RULE *n*. Further discussion of the treatment of exceptions in phonology, see Coats (1970b) and Kisseberth (1970).

[10] Trubetzkoy (1934), p. 57 fn. 42, remarks about this pair that "Der Inf. *jiti* (ETI) 'futuere' wird nur in gewissen festgeprägten Schimpfformeln gebraucht; in normaler infinitivischer Funktion gebraucht man nur *jet'* (ET'). Übrigens, ist dies ein typisches 'Tabu-Wort'." Phonologically, the alternation ETI ∼ ET' is obviously dependent on the position of stress, root-stress resulting in ET', infinitive-ending-stress resulting in ETÍ (cf. the brief discussion given in §1 above). It is interesting to note that regardless of where the stress falls, both forms must be considered irregular because the root final *b* drops before *t* of the infinitive ending; in Russian, *b* assibilates in this position, as can be seen from infinitives like GRESTI (root *greb-*), SKRESTI (root *skreb-*). The forms ETI ∼ ET' are apparently relics of an earlier Slavic period when only dentals assibilated before *t;* cf. OCS *vesti* (3 pl. *vedǫtu*), *plesti* (3 pl. *pletǫtu*) etc, but *teti* (3 pl. *tepǫtu*), *greti* (3 pl. *grebǫtu*) etc. More discussion, see Lightner (1972).

§4. THE TREATMENT OF PREFIXAL u, i

For a number of reasons it is necessary to separate a prefix from what follows by a symbol #, which corresponds roughly to a word-boundary: (1) prefixal final vowels do not drop before a vowel (NA-UK, PERE-O-XLAŽDENIE, etc.), (2) prefixal final u does not shift to w before a vowel (PODYGRAT' from $podu\#igr$; cf. *I*GRAT'), (3) Slavic roots with initial e have a prothetic glide j (EXAT' [jéxəṭ] from #exat#); prothesis does not occur before morpheme boundary (thus #nes+é+tu# ↝ #nes+jé+tu#); but prothesis does occur between prefix and root initial e, just as if this e were word-initial (DOEXAT' [dajéxəṭ] from #do#exat#). The behavior of prefixal u, i is, in part, dependent on the presence of this boundary symbol #. Prefixal u, i's display a fair amount of idiosyncracy,[11] but the general patterns seem to be as follows:

(1) prefixal u, i is always dropped before another prefix:
POD-S-KAZAT' from $podu\#su\#$ ...
RAS-S-PROSIT' from $razu\#su\#$ ...

(2) prefixal u, i is always dropped before a root which does not contain u, i:[12]
V-PISAT' from $vu\#pis$ ...
S-VOROTIT' from $su\#vort$ ...
V-BIRAT' from $vu\#bĭr$ ... (the underlying root here is bir with lax i; cf. fn. 4 above).

(3) prefixal u, i is always dropped before a root containing u, i which is not dropped:
POD-BERËT from $podu\#bir+é+t$ *(bir* is specified —DROP here*)*
RAZ-ŽËG from $razu\#žig+l+u$
OT-PÉJ from $otu\#pij+ĭ$
OT-MÓET from $otu\#muj+e+t$

---

[11] Prepositions are in principle handled like prefixes but there is even greater idiosyncracy here, and I shall not discuss this difficult problem in this paper.

[12] VOPIT' (3 pl. VOPJAT) 'to howl, wail' is from the root vop and does not have a prefix (cf. VOPL' 'howl, wail').

(4) prefixal u, i is lowered ONLY in one position: when followed by a root containing u, i which is to be dropped. From the first three roots given in (3) above, for example, are formed

PODO-BRAT' from $podu \# bir + á + t'$
RAZO-ŽGLA from $razu \# žig + l + á$
OTO-P'JET from $otu \# pij + é + tu$
note also PODO-ŽDËT from $podu \# žid + é + tu$

Since there are many environments in which prefixal u, i's are dropped and only one environment in which they are lowered, let us try to handle these prefixal VOWEL $\sim$ ZERO alternations in the following manner: a special rule first lowers prefixal u, i; all prefixal u, i which are not lowered by this rule are then dropped by rule (DROP). The problem is to find the proper environment for the prefix-lowering rule.

Since prefixal u, i are lowered only before a root containing u, i, the environment must at least be _____ $\# C \begin{Bmatrix} u \\ i \end{Bmatrix}$. Also included in this environment, however, must be the fact that the u, i in the root must drop. Since u, i drop before a syllable containing any vowel except u, i, the environment must be expanded to _____ $\# C \begin{Bmatrix} u \\ i \end{Bmatrix} C \bar{J}$, where $\bar{J}$ = any vowel except u, i. This formulation is still not satisfactory, however, because stressed $ú$, $í$ do not drop (the stressed $ú$, $í$ in $otu \# múj + e + t$ and $otu \# píj + ì$, e.g., are lowered giving OTMÓJET and OTPÉJ, resp.). Thus the environment must be restricted to _____ $\# C \begin{Bmatrix} u, i \\ \text{-stress} \end{Bmatrix} C \bar{J}$. But still the environment is not exactly correct because it does not handle cases like POD-BERÉT from $podu \# \underset{-\text{DROP}}{bir} + é + t$. In this form, the root vowel is lowered because the root is idiosyncratically specified as an exception to rule (DROP); compare PODO-ŽDËT from $podu \underset{+\text{DROP}}{\# žid} + é + t$, where the root vowel is (regularly) dropped and the prefixal u is consequently lowered. Since the prefix-lowering rule must be formulated so that the u in $podu$ is lowered before the root $\underset{+\text{DROP}}{žid}$ but not before $\underset{-\text{DROP}}{bir}$ the environment for this rule must make reference to the feature ±DROP; the rule must be formulated as follows:

(prefix-LOWER) {u, i} → {o, e} / ____ #C $\begin{bmatrix} u, i \\ -\text{stress} \\ +\text{DROP} \end{bmatrix}$ C J̄,

where J̄ = any vowel except *u* or *i*.

Representations of relevant forms are given below, and it can be seen that the three rules (prefix-LOWER), (DROP), (LOWER) — applied in that order — correctly lower or drop *u* and *i* (recall that the specification +DROP has been repressed; any *u*, *i* not marked −DROP should be read as if it were specified +DROP):

podu#su#kazát	→ POD-S-KAZAT'
vu#pisát	→ V-PISAT
podu#bir+é+t −DROP	→ POD-BERËT
razu#žíg+l+u	→ RAZ-ŽEG
otu#píj+i	→ OT-PEJ
otu#múj+e+t	→ OTMOJET
podu#birát	→ PODOBRAT
podu#žid+é+t	→ PODOŽDËT
razu#žig+l+á	→ RAZOŽGLA
otu#pij+é+t	→ OTO-P'JËT

Although this analysis "works", it is quite clearly not correct The environment of (prefix-LOWER) includes the entire rule (DROP); moreover the environment of (prefix-LOWER) includes the proposed language-independent constraint on dropping stressed vowels and the inclusion of a statement that the following root may not be an idiosyncratic exception to the following rule. If the reasoning behind the formulation of (prefix-LOWER) is correct, then the statement of the rule should be as follows:

(prefix-LOWER)'   prefixal *u*, *i* is lowered if and only if followed by a root containing *u*, *i* which will be dropped by (DROP).

But if (prefix-LOWER)' is the correct formulation of the rule governing prefixal *u*, *i*, then phonological theory must be formulated in such a way that a rule of the grammar is allowed to look ahead of itself: its application or non-application may be permitted to depend on the application or non-application of a rule that follows.

Another analysis is possible: rather than drop u, i straight away, as was done in rule (DROP), we could characterize those u, i's to be dropped by means of some special feature specification — characterize them as —VOICED, for example[13] — and then include a rule to drop voiceless vowels and a rule to lower voiced u, i. These rules would take roughly the following form:

(1)   unstressed, non-prefixal u, i are specified —*voiced* unless followed immediately by a syllable containing u, i.
(2)   prefixal u, i are specified —*voiced* unless followed immediately by a syllable containing a voiceless vowel.
(3)   voiceless vowels are dropped.
(4)   {u, i} → {o, e}

The derivations of RAZ-ŽËG, RAZO-ŽGLA, and PODO-ŽDAT' under this analysis are as follows:

```
und. repr:   razu#žíg+l+u    razu#žig+l+á    podu#žid+á+t
   (1):                         u̥                i̥              i̥
   (2):         u̥
   (3):         ∅               ∅                ∅                ∅
   (4):         é                                o                o
result:       razžég         razožglá         podoždát
```

Under this analysis, the root *bir* is specified idiosyncratically as an exception to rule (1) in the present tense, and the derivation of PODBERËT is as follows:

```
underlying representation:       podu#bir+é+t
                                    —(1)
              (1):               ——————
              (2):                   u̥
              (3):                   ∅
              (4):                         e
derived representation:          podberét
```

---

[13] I am indebted to Jeanette Gundel for this suggestion.

§5. EVALUATING THE TWO ANALYSES

In deciding how to choose between the analysis presented in §§ 2–3 and the analysis presented in § 4, it is necessary to examine the motivation behind the competing linguistic theories.

The proponent of the voiceless vowel theory would presumably claim that the theory of phonology advocated by Chomsky and Halle, and their followers — in particular the constraints on rule ordering — is sufficiently powerful to account for phonological phenomena found in languages of the world. The choice of the feature ±VOICED — instead of, say, ±NASALIZED, ±PHARYNGALIZED, or some equally unlikely feature — will be defended on the basis of the fact that there are reasonably well-documented languages with voiceless vowels which drop. Thus, for example, lax *i*, *u* under certain conditions may be pronounced voiceless in Japanese, and some of these voiceless vowels may optionally be dropped.[14]

One might try to rectify the necessity of referring to UNSTRESSED vowels in rule (1) by proposing a language-independent condition that stressed vowels may not be specified —VOICED, but such a proposal seems incorrect in view of such Japanese forms with voiceless, stressed, high-pitched vowels as k_i^+ta 'came', s_i^+ku 'four times nine', and so on.

The proponent of the analysis which permits the grammar to look ahead of itself will presumably argue against the voiceless vowel analysis by claiming that the resulting derivations are artificial (perhaps because one never finds voiceless [u̥] or [i̥] in phonetic representations in Russian). This theory will claim that a simple linear ordering of rules is not a sufficiently powerful device to capture the relevant generalizations to be found in languages of the world. Kisseberth (1971) presents examples in which the grammar must "look behind itself": in order to capture a generalization, a rule must be formulated that applies not merely to the output of the immediately preceding rule but which must be permitted to look back at the shape of the string BEFORE the preceding rule applied.

University of Texas, Austin

---

[14] Actually, the situation here is a bit more complex than suggested in the text; brief discussion, see Lightner (1970), pp. 180–181 and esp. p. 215 fn 5.

REFERENCES

Coats, Herbert S.
   1970a "The Assignment of Stress in Modern Russian" (unpublished PhD dissertation, University of Illinois).
   1970b "Rule Environment Features in Phonology", *Papers in Linguistics* 2 (1), 110–140.

Kisseberth, Charles W.
   1970 "The Treatment of Exceptions", *Papers in Linguistics* 2 (1), 45–58.
   1971 "Klamath Phonology", *Studies in Honor of Renée and Henry Kahane* (University of Illinois Press).

Lightner, Theodore M.
   1966 "On the Phonology of Old Church Slavonic Conjugation", *IJSLP* X, 1–28.
   1969 "On the Alternation $e \sim o$ in Modern Russian", *Linguistics* 54, 44–69.
   1970 "Why and How Does Vowel Nasalization Take Place?" *Papers in Linguistics* 2 (2), 179–226.
   1972 *Problems in the Theory of Phonology: Russian Phonology and Turkish Phonology* (Linguistic Research, Inc.: Edmonton, Alberta, Canada).

Trubetzkoy, Nikolaj
   1934 *Das morphonologische System der russischen Sprache* = *TCLP* 5 (deuxième partie).

PART TWO

LITERATURE

THE WRITER AS WITNESS:
THE ACHIEVEMENT OF ALEXANDER SOLZHENITSYN

VICTOR ERLICH

A recent visitor to the Soviet Union, fortunate enough to meet and befriend some nonconformist Russian intellectuals, will almost invariably find in the homes of his hosts three literary icons. These are Anna Axmatova, Boris Pasternak and Alexander Solzhenitsyn.

Solzhenitsyn is the only surviving member of the trinity and the only representative of prose-fiction in this heterodox literary pantheon. For thousands of literate men and women all over Russia he is the conscience of modern Russian literature, a moral force, a culture hero. More than a mere writer, one may be tempted to say. The phrase, however, would be misleading: Solzhenitsyn's moral authority derives primarily from his being a writer, more exactly from being the kind of writer he chose and dared to be.

An attempt to assess the literary accomplishment of a novelist of such stature and resonance is inevitably a humbling and a precarious task. As is so often the case in dealing with recent Soviet literature, literary and moral-political considerations are so closely intertwined here as to be virtually inseparable. When, as readers of *One Day in the Life of Ivan Denisovich*, we confront the belated revelation of a long-denied nightmare, "no sane person", to quote Irving Howe, "can be expected to register a purely literary response".[1]

What is called for, I submit, is not literary purism, but respect for the autonomy of literary criteria. Our admiration for the man and our affinity for his stance need not determine our considered judgment of the scope and the texture of the writer's achievement. A moving human testimony couched in fictional terms may or may not be a literary masterpiece. At the same time, we would do

---

[1] Irving Howe, "Predicaments of Soviet Writing", I, *The New Republic* (May 12, 1963).

well to beware of the opposite danger, that of inhibiting our literary response, of underestimating the heroic writer's actual effectiveness out of an excessive distrust of our own motives, an inordinate fear of being or appearing to be swayed by extra-literary considerations.

Let me mention another difficulty which seems to beset a Western critic of fiction in dealing with Solzhenitsyn. His conceptual apparatus, attuned as it is to the post-modern sophistication of Nabokov and Borges, John Barth and Nathalie Sarraute, is likely to grind to a halt in the face of a novelist so sturdily and expansively old fashioned, so steeped in the 19th-century realistic tradition, so unself-conscious about the "point of view" as to insert casually into a section of his major novel which reconstructs a protagonist's past largely in his own terms an unabashedly explicit authorial generalization: "He [Rubin, V. E.] was all-in-all a tragic figure."[2]

This uneasiness, this uncertainty of criteria, may account in part for a freakishly wide range of responses to Solzhenitsyn in American criticism. In an early reaction,[3] Franklin D. Reeve hailed *One Day in the Life of Ivan Denisovich* as one of the greatest works of 20th-century European literature, more accomplished than Thomas Mann's *Death in Venice* or André Gide's *The Counterfeiters*. Several years later, in discussing Solzhenitsyn's longest and most ambitious novel, *The First Circle*, Robert Garis adjudged him a mediocre if "honorable" writer.[4] Strangely enough, both Reeve and Garis went out of their way to play down the topicality of Solzhenitsyn's work. Mr. Reeve contended that *One Day* was "really" not about a Soviet forced labor camp, but about a man's search for himself. Mr. Garis claimed that Solzhenitsyn's social criticism could have been directed with equal force against "any" society. I am tempted to suggest that this curious convergence between otherwise so disparate assessments points to another pitfall of modern criticism — notably its occasional preference for the fanciful over the "obvious". The latter, in this case, might be couched in an unexciting, but, I believe, correct proposition that, while the import of Solzhenitsyn's fiction clearly transcends its immediate setting, much of his authority and persuasiveness derives from his immersion in Soviet reality, his unerring sense of the characteristically, if not always uniquely,

---

[2] *V kruge pervom* (Paris: YMCA Press, 1969), 477.
[3] "The House of Living", *The Kenyon Review* (Spring 1963), 356–360.
[4] "Fiction Chronicle", *The Hudson Review* (April 1969), 148–154.

Soviet institutional patterns, of the characteristically, if not always uniquely, Russian modes of repression and protest, of depravity and integrity.

But I am getting ahead of my story. It is high time that we stop worrying about the critics' dilemmas, whether real or imaginary, and confront our subject.

It is symbolic of Solzhenitsyn's place in modern Russian literature that he should have begun his career as a taboo-breaker. In his momentous debut, *One Day in the Life of Ivan Denisovich* (1962), a dread institution whose existence had hitherto been ignored or timidly hinted at by an Erenburg, a Dudincev, or a Viktor Nekrasov was suddenly catapulted into public view. The grim routine of what a French writer, David Rousset, had called "l'univers concentrationnaire", the unspeakable squalor and misery, the backbreaking labor, the animal scrounging for food, is authenticated here by a wealth of detail and made more credible by the author's quiet, undramatic manner. *One Day* is not a horror story. Physical violence appears in the novel not as a central actuality, but as an everpresent threat. When the shivering, hungry inmates start their forced march, the guards load their rifles: any false step will mean death.

The long, grueling sequence from reveille to "lights-out" chronicled in Solzhenitsyn's unhurried narrative represents an ordinary, in fact, a relatively "lucky" day in the life of the tale's goodnatured protagonist who, even in the forced labor camp inferno, takes pride in a job well done. As the story draws to its close, Ivan Denisovich muses thus: "He had had a lot of luck today . . . they hadn't put him in the cooler. He had finagled an extra bowl of mush at noon . . . nothing had spoiled the day, and it had been almost happy . . .".[5]

Though technically *One Day* is a third-person narrative, the point of view is provided here by a "simple" peasant whose potential for survival is greater than his ratiocinative powers. This device, skillfully and consistently employed, is both a strength and a built-in limitation. The language of *One Day* — an effective blend of the earthy peasant vernacular with the harsh camp jargon which occasionally lapses into profanity — is a far cry from the colorless,

One Day in the Life of Ivan Denisovich (New York: Frederick A. Praeger, 1963), 209–210.

timidly puritan prose of "socialist-realist" fiction. It is also testimony to Solzhenitsyn's sturdy sense of style — a quality which, of late, has not been much in evidence in Soviet fiction. Yet the sustained "folksy" stylization which lends solidity and color to the verbal texture of *One Day*, constricts the story's scope and import and obviates the need for, indeed eliminates the possibility of, an articulate judgment on the life presented.

Solzhenitsyn's keen ear for the leisurely rhythms of Russian folk speech stands him in good stead in a story which, to my mind, is his most accomplished work to date, "Matrëna's Home" (1963). The narrator, who, not unlike the author, is a former political prisoner and a teacher, decides to "cut loose and get lost in the innermost heart of Russia, if there is any such thing".[6] The phrase seems to suggest a hankering for some traditional Russian ambience. In fact, both the language and the moral tenor of "Matrëna's Home" have a strikingly old-fashioned quality. The central figure of the story, a selfless, gentle, pure-of-heart peasant woman, makes one think of the quiet radiance of that chastened village belle, Lukerja, in Turgenev's "The Living Relic". When Matrëna dies, a victim, symbolically, of her neighbor's brutal, unthinking acquisitiveness, the narrator is moved to comment: "We all lived beside her and never understood that she was the righteous one, without whom no village can stand, nor any city. Nor our homeland."[7]

None of this was likely to please the official critics. Owing to Khrushchev's personal *imprimatur*, *One Day* enjoyed initially a measure of immunity, but "Matrëna's Home" was fair game. The story was promptly attacked for offering a distorted picture of the Soviet village. Did the author fail to realize that such "capitalistic" attitudes as competitiveness and greed had long ago disappeared from the Soviet countryside? Nor was Solzhenitsyn's positive message — clearly at odds with the "struggle"-oriented and stridently public Soviet ethos — any less objectionable.

It is a matter of record that neither of Solzhenitsyn's full-length novels was allowed publication in his native land. The writer whom many Russians regard, in Yevtushenko's phrase, as "our only living classic", has been forced underground. Was this due to the deterioration of the Soviet cultural climate since Khrushchev?

[6] "Matrënin dvor", A. Solženicyn, *Sočinenija* (Posev, 1966), 195.
[7] *Ibid.*, 231.

While the fact itself is undeniable, in all fairness to present-day Russia's dour-faced bosses, there is little reason to assume that either *Cancer Ward* or *The First Circle* would have received a nod from the more ebullient Nikita Khrushchev.

A Western critic, mindful of the larger thrust of Solzhenitsyn's fiction and conditioned to symbol-hunting, may be tempted to construe *Cancer Ward* as a parable for a deadly disease which had eaten its way into the Soviet body politic.[8] This temptation ought to be resisted. *Cancer Ward* is a sturdily realistic novel rather than an allegory. It appears to be a thoroughly reliable and accurate portrayal of a "real" cancer ward in a "real" hospital in Soviet Central Asia. Characteristically, the impression of authenticity owes at least as much to the apparent mastery of the *realia* — the density of the relevant medical detail — as it does to the biographical fact of Solzhenitsyn's actually having had a bout with lung cancer. Yet it is hardly necessary to insist that the novel has wider, non-medical implications. The motif of an incurable or seemingly incurable illness serves here as a mode of revealing character and impelling a verdict over the meaning or meaninglessness of a doomed life. The nearly inescapable parallel with Leo Tolstoy's masterly "Death of Ivan Il'ich" has already been drawn.[9] While the affinity between the two works is undeniable, one of the significant differences is that while in Tolstoy the moment of truth dramatizes the terrible emptiness of an "ordinary" life — Ivan Il'ich is Everyman! — in Solzhenitsyn the ultimate confrontation is a *sui generis* projective test designed to elicit a variety of character-and-status-determined responses.

Already in this, the less ambitious of his two major novels, Solzhenitsyn demonstrates his remarkable ability to encompass within a confining institutional framework a galaxy of richly differentiated character studies. Here is a successful Stalinist bureaucrat Rusanov, appalled at being thrown together with the "common people" whom he presumably serves, blithely assuming that each morning he

---

[8] For obvious reasons, the above interpretation was eagerly adopted by some of Solzhenitsyn's Soviet detractors. At a November 17, 1966, meeting of the Artistic Prose Division of the Soviet Writer's Union, one N. Asanov meandered ominously: "Cancerous growth, incurability of cancer ... suppose what is meant here is not an individual, but [our] society?" (*Novyj Žurnal*, No. 93 [New York, 1968], 229).

[9] See especially Deming Brown, "*Cancer Ward* and *The First Circle*", *Slavic Review* (June 1969), 304–313.

ought to be the first to get the newspaper, not only because he is an important person, but because he alone is able to decipher the arcane language of the Party edicts; a smug dignitary whose arrogance is visibly eroded by the inexorable progress of his illness and his mounting dependency on the hospital staff and his fellow patients. Here is a dedicated young geologist, racing against time for the sake of the only thing that matters to him — a scientific breakthrough which he feels he alone is capable of effecting; a tough, unscrupulous operator, deeply stirred by the reading of Leo Tolstoy's parable "What Do Men Live By?" and, characteristically, unable to share his excitement and his belated soul-searching either with the cliché-ridden Party hack or the single-track-minded scientist. A former labor camp inmate Kostoglotov, intransigent and blunt to the point of rudeness, who in a heated exchange with Rusanov, calls him a "racist" for judging people by their social origins rather than by what they are or do. Finally there is a haggard ex-academician whose physical misery is compounded by a crushing sense of guilt over having been silent while the best of his contemporaries were vilified, tortured and annihilated.

In his relentless integrity, his past ordeals and his current difficulties of "readjustment", Oleg Kostoglotov comes closest to being the author's counterpart as well as the hero of the novel. His intimate entanglements — a timid yet urgent romance, poignantly undercut by medical treatment which threatens his sexual potency — are handled with empathy and tact. Yet interestingly enough, it is the guilt-ridden ex-conformist Šulubin who is entrusted with articulating as positive a moral-political vision as any found in the Solzhenitsyn *oeuvre* — a vision of "ethical socialism",[10] of a "society in which all relationships, principles and laws would be based on morality and on nothing else".[11]

---

[10] Characteristically, Šulubin insists on labeling his brand of socialism as ethical or moral *(nravstvennyj)* rather than "Christian" or "democratic". Though the good society that he envisions is to be built on love rather than on hate, the slogan of "Christian Socialism" strikes him as too pat and "too far removed from reality". By the same token, the phrase "democratic socialism" is discarded as overly procedural and essentially negative. The word "democratic", maintains Šulubin, "does not describe the nature of socialism, but its form, a kind of institutional set-up. But this is just a declaration ... that heads won't roll, but nothing is said about what this socialism will be built on." (p. 370).

[11] *Rakovyj korpus* (Paris: YMCA Press, 1968), 371.

The attribution of what can be assumed to be the author's own social ideals to — if I may paraphrase a current cliché — a member of Stalinist Russia's "silent majority", a man, who unlike Solzhenitsyn or Kostoglotov, had failed the test of courage, is a singularly compassionate, non-vindictive gesture. Moreover, Šulubin's credo suggests an important Solzhenitsyn theme — that of a man's ability to think heterodox thoughts while bowing to outward pressures, an ability which no amount of repression, short of one's actual annihilation, can totally inhibit or destroy. "Tell me", asks Kostoglotov, "did you think of this during those twenty-five years when you were bowing low and renouncing your beliefs?" "Yes, I did", answers Šulubin, "I renounced everything and I went on thinking. I stuffed the books into the stove and I kept thinking. Why not? Haven't I earned the right to a few thoughts through my sufferings, through my betrayal?"[12]

The motif of inward freedom which "they" cannot take away from you reappears in a different key in Solzhenitsyn's most broadly conceived work, whose title is drawn from Dante's "Inferno", *The First Circle*. In Solzhenitsyn's fictional universe "hell" is the Soviet forced labor camp system. Its "first circle", its upper stratum, is the technical research institute on the outskirts of Moscow, whose employees — top-flight scientists, engineers and mechanics — are brought from the lower circles of the inferno in order to work feverishly on high-priority security assignments. The "project", which provides the core of the bulky narrative, is a concerted effort to evolve a technique whereby a minute acoustic analysis of a tapped telephone conversation could yield the speaker's identity. The "privileged" victims of a totalitarian regime are compelled thus to strain their intelligence and skills in order to entrap others into the fatal net. The tragic irony of the situation is compounded by the fact that some of the more dedicated researchers-inmates are propelled not merely by a fear of returning to the pit, but also by a misplaced intellectual zest and residual Party loyalty.

The central plot of this wide-ranging novel, encased in three frenzied and fateful days, is that of a chilling technological suspense story. On December 24, 1949, Innokenty Volodin, an up-and-coming young Soviet diplomat, makes a call from a public booth: he is trying to warn an eminent Soviet physician whom he has known

[12] *Ibid.*, 372.

since childhood against sharing a medical discovery with his French colleagues and thus walking into a trap laid for him. The conversation is intercepted. Two days later, an enthusiastic philologist, turned acoustician in the elite prison-institute, breathlessly announces a breakthrough on the voice-identification "front". In a matter of hours, Volodin lands in the dread Moscow jail Lubjanka: a dignitary is reduced to an unperson . . .

It is a tribute to Solzhenitsyn's novelistic skill that working out of so narrow a base, he manages, by making full use of the inmates' links with the outside world, to bring into the compass of his narrative various strata of Soviet society — security officials, diplomats, writers, students. The cumulative effect is as panoramic a vision of Stalinist Russia as any found in recent Soviet literature.

The picture of the Soviet system which emerges from Solzhenitsyn's narrative is as credible as it is terrifying.[13] It is a bureaucratic spiral of fear: everybody, from the boss of the secret police through the head of the "research institute" and its divisional directors down to the prison guard, is terrorized, for everybody's career and life are literally "on the line". A blunder, a failure to meet a typically unrealistic deadline, can easily prove irreversible.

This pyramid of terror is capped by the Leader, a devious, vindictive, pathologically suspicious and grubbily lonely tyrant. The Stalin sequence in *The First Circle* has come in for vigorous criticism. It has been found jarring, if not self-indulgent, a lapse into pamphleteering, an obtrusion of loaded speculation upon a well-authenticated testimony. These strictures have some validity. Solzhenitsyn's Stalin — though, to my mind, credible enough — lacks the authority and the depth of his best characterizations. Occasional intrusion of heavy sarcasm, of *de facto* editorializing, into a reconstruction of Stalin's nighttime thoughts, represents a discernible shift in tone and style. (The importance of this "lapse" can be easily overestimated. A vaster and more resonant work than *One Day*, *The First Circle* fails to achieve, or for that matter, to aim at, the degree of stylistic unity which characterized Solzhenitsyn's compact début.) Yet the implication that the Stalin chapters are a foreign body in Solzhenitsyn's fictional universe strikes me as totally false. Whatever their shortcomings, they represent an organic, perhaps an indis-

---

[13] In a lecture recently delivered at Yale, Hannah Arendt maintains that *The First Circle* ought to be required reading for students of totalitarianism.

pensable, element of the novel's structure, not only because the picture of the sytem would not have been complete without its pivot, but, and more importantly, because Solzhenitsyn's conception of Stalin is an essential aspect of the moral dialectics which informs *The First Circle*.

Though the theme of incarceration dominates the world of Solzhenitsyn, the rather platitudinous, if not altogether erroneous, notion of Stalin's Russia as one big prison is *not* the central, let alone the distinctive, insight here. What confronts us is a seeming moral paradox: only in prison can one be really free. Only those who, like Neržin, Bobynin, Xorobrov, have nothing to lose since they have already lost everything — influence, power, material possessions, often their loved ones — can maintain their basic humanity, their personal dignity, their ability to act upon the dictates of their consciences.[14] But if only the powerless can be brave, it stands to reason that the Omnipotent Leader should be the most fearful of them all. Thus, rather than being a gratuitous discharge of the author's pent-up rage, the image of Stalin's free-floating paranoia completes the moral equation which is central to the novel. It eminently belongs in the picture.

Though not a flawless work, *The First Circle* is a compelling literary performance. To have launched a multi-level and many-voiced novel through the medium of a fateful "phone call", and, having plausibly and dramatically intertwined so many individual destinies, to have brought the narrative back to its starting point in the powerful scene of Volodin's arrest, one of the most memorable passages in modern Russian literature, is eloquent testimony to Solzhenitsyn's compositional resources and narrative gifts. By the same token, it is a tribute to Solzhenitsyn's powers of characterization that both the novel's chief protagonist, Gleb Neržin, and his loving adversary, Lev Rubin, should be so thoroughly convincing, so richly credible.

Solzhenitsyn succeeds where many creditable novelists have failed. In Neržin he has created a "positive hero" who dispenses

---

[14] Bobynin states the matter forcefully in the course of a confrontation with the sinister Man of Power, the head of the MGB, Abakumov: "I have nothing, you understand, nothing ! You can't get my wife or child — a bomb got them first. My parents are already dead. All I own is my handkerchief . . . you took my freedom away long ago. What else can you threaten me with ? What else can you deprive me of? . . ." (p. 183).

with false heroics, an author's *alter ego* who is not an ideological vehicle but a fully realized human being. A humanist who, in his journey through hell, has jettisoned his illusions but not his values, a thinking man who sets more store by experience than by ideology, an intellectual who is free of intellectual pride,[15] a mathematician who, in a quixotic gesture, foregoes the rewards of the relative security of a strenuous cryptographic project in order to keep himself available to reflection, to "learning about life" on one of the lowest rungs of the labor camp inferno, Neržin is one of the few truly satisfying portrayals of an honorable man in modern literature.

If Neržin is a triumph of objectified introspection, Lev Rubin is a feat of empathy for the "Other". A life-loving doctrinaire, a brilliant and erudite scholar who, after all his ordeals, persists in speaking about Stalin in terms of uncritical adulation, an honest and warm-hearted man betrayed by a mixture of intellectual exuberance and misguided patriotism into tightening a noose on the neck of an unsuspecting victim, Lev Rubin as a fictional creation bears witness to Solzhenitsyn's compassion and to his keen awareness of the tragic complexity of human motives.

As one surveys Solzhenitsyn's fictional universe, from Ivan Denisovič's struggle for "an extra bowl of mush" down to Neržin's brief and tense prison meeting with his wife, the overarching impression, the salient quality is that of relentless veracity. No other living Russian writer has earned as fully as did Solzhenitsyn the right to echo the young Tolstoy's famous credo and battlecry: "The real

---

[15] Therein lies a significant difference between Neržin and another appealing protagonist of *The First Circle*, Sologdin. A brilliant and proud man, a relentless challenger of orthodox pieties which Rubin seeks to uphold, Sologdin is the most articulate non-conformist in *The First Circle*. In one of his confrontations with Rubin he clearly speaks for the author as he exclaims: "The higher the ends the higher must be the means!... Morality shouldn't lose force as it increases its scope!" (p. 469). And yet it is at least arguable that in the end Sologdin's intellectual pride subverts his intransigence. Since his superiors desperately need Sologdin's problem-solving talents, he turns the tables on them! Instead of grovelling and begging for favors, the powerless prisoner confronts the powers-that-be with an ultimatum. He wins, but only at the cost of agreeing to play the game, which the less flamboyant Neržin firmly refuses to do.

hero of my tale, whom I love with all the force of my soul ... is Truth."[16]

Yet, one might interpose, is not the parallel with one of the world's literary giants precisely the kind of extravagant overestimate against which I was cautioning in my opening remarks? Not necessarily. It is a legitimate tribute to the moral force and the literary solidity of Solzhenitsyn's *oeuvre* that the parallel should suggest itself so readily. By the same token, it is no reflection on the import and the genuineness of his attainment to urge that the analogy not be pressed too far. (How many distinguished novelists could stand this comparison without being diminished by it?) A standard reaction to a Solzhenitsyn character or incident is "yes, that's the way it must have been", "yes, that's the way people — or this particular kind of person — act under stress". Yet when Tolstoy describes Levin's and Kitty's honeymoon, the "truth" about personal relations acquires the force of a moral jolt, of an unsettling epiphany. To put it differently, it is obvious, at least to me, that Solzhenitsyn is a *major* writer. Yet if "greatness" in literature spells transcendent moral illumination and/or an esthetic breakthrough, this quality may have to be denied to Solzhenitsyn as it would have to be denied, I believe, to any other living novelist.

A final distinction: in Solzhenitsyn, as in Tolstoy, "truth" is both an avowed ideal and a polemical strategy, a challenge to the *idées reçues*. Yet their lines of attack are different. An iconoclast of genius, Tolstoy had set out to dislodge the extant fictional modes of seeing and portraying reality. His leitmotif, to quote the brilliant Formalist critic Boris Ejxenbaum,[17] was "it is not" what you think *(ne to)*. War is not what you think ("The Sebastopol Stories", *War and Peace*). Love is not what you think *(Family Happiness)*. History is not what you think *(War and Peace)*.

Solzhenitsyn's immediate targets are not literary conventions grown stale, but externally imposed and enforced taboos and clichés. The task that fell to him, at the peak of the post-Stalin literary thaw, was no less significant for being more "elementary". For in a situation where, to paraphrase his own words, "many an author [who] saw and touched the truth ... lied with cold glassy eyes",[18]

[16] "Sevastopol' v mae", L. Tolstoj, *Sobranie sočinenij* 2 (Moscow, 1958), 158.
[17] *Molodoj Tolstoj* (Petrograd–Berlin, 1922).
[18] *V kruge pervom*, 198.

calling a spade a spade, naming the unnameable, was a liberating act. To establish a reliable connection between words and things, between language and the facts of experience, is to recreate the essential conditions of a genuine literary enterprise, to restore to Russian literature mired in ready-made formulae, in melodramatic stereotypes, its proper role, its natural function, that of search, exploration, and above all, testimony.

Let me cite in closing a poignant passage from *Cancer Ward*, a conversation between Kostoglotov and another former labor camp inmate, a cultivated, middle-aged woman reduced to the status of a hospital orderly. She speaks with bitterness about her daughter's shedding tears over *Anna Karenina*. To Elizaveta Anatol'evna Anna's fate is almost enviable: she made a choice and paid the price. How about us, she asks in an anguished whisper. How about millions whose lives were destroyed or maimed by police arbitrariness? "Where can I read about us? In a hundred years?"[19]

Thanks to Solzhenitsyn, she did not have to wait that long: he has heeded her call. In his fiction, the speechless have found a voice, the dispossessed a home. To have borne witness to the truth in the teeth of mounting persecution is an act of moral courage unsurpassed in this or any other era. To have done so on a scale and in a manner commensurate with the magnitude of the subject, is one of the major literary achievements of our time.

Yale University

---

[19] *Rakovyj korpus*, p. 402.

THE GOGOL PROBLEM: PERSPECTIVES FROM ABSENCE

DONALD FANGER

"Truly", Gogol wrote his mother shortly before his nineteenth birthday, "I am considered a riddle by everyone ... At home they consider me capricious, some kind of unbearable pedant who thinks he is smarter than anyone, that he has been created differently from other people ... Here [at school] they call me humble, the ideal of meekness and patience. In one place I am the most quiet, modest, courteous; in another, melancholy, pensive, uncouth, etc.; in a third, garrulous ... with some clever, with others stupid ... Consider me what you will, *but only once I have embarked on my real career will you come to know my true character.*"[1]

Fourteen years later, he had more than embarked on his real career. He was now famous as the author of *Dead Souls, The Inspector General*, and all the artistic work he was to publish in his lifetime. Indeed, he said he had "no life outside literature" — by which he meant outside the projected volumes that would complete *Dead Souls*. But the answer was now postponed. Only the completion of the novel, he said, "will finally solve the riddle of my existence" (XII, 58). Ten years later, most of the long-promised, once- (perhaps twice-) burned manuscript of Volume II was burned again (by mistake, he said); ten years of the life (excepting one fiasco, *Selected Passages from Correspondence with Friends*, which needed to be redeemed by the progress of *Dead Souls*) were cancelled; and his death, clearly not without suicidal intent, followed quickly. The riddle of his existence thus remained, in the sense that the work which was to crown it and show the sense of its evolution was missing.

He did, it is true, hint at least at a partial answer which he said

---

[1] N. V. Gogol', *Polnoe sobranie sočinenij* X (Akademija Nauk SSSR, 1937–1952), 123. All subsequent references to Gogol's writings are to this edition and included in parentheses in the text.

he had prepared as a posthumous gift to his fellow-countrymen. *Selected Passages* opens with a testament, and there he wills them "the best of all the things that my pen has produced, . . . my composition entitled 'A Farewell Tale' *(Proščal'naja povest')*". It would reveal to them "if only in part the strict secret of life and the most sacred heavenly music of that secret". He was reserving publication, he explained in a footnote, because "what could have significance after [the writer's] death has no sense during [his] lifetime" (VIII, 220-222). "A Farewell Tale" was apparently never written — and Dostoevsky did not hesitate to brand Gogol's references to it as *vran'e* — prevarication. Gogol, he suggested, here and elsewhere, was an early version of his own "underground man".[2]

When Gogol died in 1852, there was a general sense that a greatness had passed from the scene — a greatness whose explanation lay in the future. Ivan Aksakov said as much in an obituary notice that alarmed the Minister of National Education: "A great deal of time must still pass", he wrote, *"before all the deep and weighty significance* of Gogol is fully understood — Gogol, that artist-monk, Christian-satirist, ascetic and humorist, *that martyr of the exalted ideal and the unsolved riddle"*. Why, the Minister complained in a secret letter, should so much time be necessary to grasp Gogol's significance fully? "Can the writer of this article really think that this significance is so unfathomable that none of our contemporaries is in a position to form a clear understanding of Gogol from his works? *And why is such a deep and weighty significance attributed primarily to Gogol?"*[3]

The mystery was vexing — and persistent. In 1909 one of the most brilliant and perceptive of all Gogol's critics (and the one who, of all, examined his texts most closely) declared categorically: "We still do not know what Gogol is" *(My ešče ne znaem, čto takoe Gogol')*.[4]

---

[2] In a manuscript of the early 1870's, Dostoevsky speaks of "that same underground nature, which made Gogol, in a solemn testament, speak of a final tale which had sung itself out of his soul — and which in reality did not exist at all". Dostoevsky goes on to suggest that when Gogol began writing his testament he may not even have known that he was about to mention a "final tale". V. V. Vinogradov, *O jazyke xudožestvennoj literatury* (Moscow, 1959), 398—399.

[3] A. S. Nikolaev and Ju. G. Oksman, eds., *Literaturnyj Muzeum* I (Petersburg, 1922), 98. Emphasis added.

[4] Andrej Belyj, "Gogol", in his *Lug zelenyj* (Moscow, 1910), 95.

That statement, I submit, remains true today.

The volume of Gogol studies — articles and books in Russian and in all the European languages — is enormous, but most of it tends, reductively, to emphasize some one aspect of the complex phenomenon at the expense of the rest. Did Gogol portray vulgar Russian types and common Russian objects? Then he must be "the poet of reality". And not only that, but a writer who is "true to life to the last degree". Thus Belinsky, whose approach and conclusions have been matter for quotation and exegesis, voluntary and involuntary, ever since — so that even now an American or west European, reacting in disgust, can hardly bring himself to consider what "social" might mean in connection with Gogol's work, let alone why intelligent people could once have wanted to call him a "realist". Instead, we prefer to cite the resolutely antisocial Nabokov, who finds in his influential little book that "fancy is only fertile when it is futile", and not only emphasizes (which is easy) but exaggerates (which is difficult) the oddity of both the man ("the oddest man in Russia") and the work.[5]

Such reactions continue to keep Gogol criticism off balance. In some sense the victim of history during his lifetime, he has remained a victim of history ever since. From which it follows that the historical dimension of the Gogol problem — albeit in need of reformulation and new approaches — must necessarily be an important one. Just how is what I shall attempt to suggest. The problem is vast, and my emphasis will be selective, if not arbitrary. But I shall try throughout to keep one eye on methodology.

The Gogol phenomenon itself is elusive partly for intrinsic reasons — and if we look at the works themselves, we find that they are not only often enigmatic when taken severally, but that as a body they tend to be intractable. His genius, that is to say, was for the fragmentary, the grotesquely proportioned and the unresolved, and this can be seen not only in particular productions, but in his *oeuvre* as a whole. One can hardly speak fruitfully of periods in his work, for example, or hope to clarify much by approaching him in terms of creative development.

---

[5] Vladimir Nabokov, *Nikolai Gogol* (Norfolk, Conn., 1944), 76, 12, and *passim*.

To be sure, his first published work and his last, separated by eighteen years, are as different from each other as they could be; but they also stand radically apart from the bulk of his central achievement. *Hanz Küchelgarten*, published in 1829, is a long, jejune poem subtitled "An Idyll in Pictures"; *Selected Passages* (1847) is a patchwork of moral, social and literary essays, couched in epistolary form and offered after five years of silence to a public clamorous for the promised second volume of *Dead Souls*. *Selected Passages* is rather more complex than the view of it that became traditional after Belinsky's impassioned rebuttal, and it has been unjustly neglected by literary critics. But the point here is that each of these works in its own way represented a blind alley for Gogol, a mistaking of his essential talent.

Leaving them aside, then, we find that all the rest of Gogol's writings were published in an intensely productive eleven-year period, from 1831 to 1842. Of these, the years 1831–1836 (up to his departure from Russia) are the years of greatest variety; here he tries his hand at all the forms of prose then being practiced: short stories from an operatic Ukrainian past (*Evenings on a Farm near Dikanka*, 1831–1832); continued in *Mirgorod* (1835); essays — lyrical, historical, esthetic, pedagogical — most of them collected in *Arabesques* (1835); stories from contemporary Russian life (some in *Arabesques*, some in periodicals); book reviews and literary journalism of a very high order; stage comedies (*The Inspector General*, early drafts of *Marriage*, several fragments); not to mention weighty works on history (Ukrainian and universal), and geography.[6] From 1836 to 1842, he eschews journalism and concentrates almost exclusively on *Dead Souls* (as well as on reworking some of his earlier pieces for the Collected Works of 1842–1843); his novel and "The Overcoat" are the masterpieces of these years, and quite overshadow the few narrative and dramatic efforts, most of them fragmentary, to which he also turned. He was twenty-two when the first volume of *Evenings* came out and made his reputation as a writer; he was thirty-three when *Dead Souls* and the *Collected*

---

[6] None of the latter seems actually to have been undertaken. But his announced interest in this kind of writing was more than grandiloquence. He did finish the draft of a textbook of literary forms in 1845 (see *PSS*, *VIII*, 468–88), and was still collecting materials for works on geography and lexicography late in his life.

Works were published, and his slow, silent, self-inflicted martyrdom began.

Clearly he did develop but the process of that development (as opposed to the direction) is not clear, because of his working habits. "He did not move", as one of his critics observes, "from one work to another but rather, as it were, in a single drawn-out moment embraced at once the whole sum of his artistic ideas — and then, fitfully turning now to one project, now to another, returning again to the early ones and at the same time polishing the new ones, suddenly appeared to history entire, in all his greatness."[7]

Other conventional lines of approach are hardly more rewarding. The vexed question of his literary filiations, for example, is the subject of an enormous monograph by a man whose surname — Čudakov — seems to vouch for his qualifications in something like the way the name of a student of Dickens' style — Randolph Quirk — does for his.[8] (Čudakov might be rendered as Mr. Eccentric.) For all the painstaking scholarship that has gone into the question, however, the fact is that there are few clear facts. We know Gogol was familiar with the work of the Russian poets of his time — but he was a prose writer. We know that he read Richardson's *Clarissa*, because he says so in a letter; we know that he read a novel by Dickens in 1840 or 1841, because a Moscow professor caught him in the act in a Roman café. But we have no reactions to either of these — and, with respect to the foreigners from whom he said he drew inspiration, no evidence of first-hand knowledge at all.[9] His 1,500-odd letters have much to say about his moods, ambitions and fluctuating creativity — but almost nothing about literature itself, Russian or foreign, in practice or in theory. Despite the similarities which Helen Muchnic has noted, then, he is no Flaubert with respect to the articulations of artistic consciousness; for his correspondence hardly allows us to form any picture of his reading,

---

[7] G. A. Gukovskij, *Realizm Gogolja* (Moscow–Leningrad, 1959), 25.

[8] G. I. Čudakov, *Otnošenie tvorčestva Gogolja k zapadno-evropejskim literaturam* (Kiev, 1908). The author provides a detailed list of what Gogol might have read, but is constantly obliged to introduce his assertions with such phrases as "one may assume".

[9] In a draft of *Dead Souls*, Chapter XI, he mentions looking up from his desk occasionally, to regard the portraits hanging on his wall — "of Shakespeare, Ariosto, Fielding, Cervantes, Pushkin, who reflected nature as it was, and not as someone or other may have wished it to be". *PSS*, VI, 533.

knowledge, tastes, or even specific awareness of literature.[10] As a result, these areas remain all but empty categories, among so many others in the Gogol phenomenon.

As for the temperament and the life, the more scrupulous the attempt to deal descriptively with them, the likelier it is to be studded with question marks, pock-marked with perhapses, and all but vitiated by conscience-induced gaps. The man was secretive, and though alarmed at what he took to be misinterpretations of his work, he did little to help his contemporaries understand its novelty or what he took to be his intentions. Those whom he did admit to a kind of intimacy found themselves, so to speak, in small rooms that did not communicate; thus the most useful memoirs — Aksakov's, Annenkov's, Smirnova's — give convincing but often contrasting pictures, and the key that would reconcile them is missing. One side of this problem may be illuminated by two categorical statements Gogol made on the subject of sincerity, together with one probable example of it. "You will believe my sincere feelings, won't you?" he writes to Raevskaja on 25 June 1840: "I do not know how to lie" (XI, 290). On 14 December 1844, however, in a revealing passage, he confesses to Shevyrev: "I have absolutely never been able to speak frankly about myself" (XII, 394) — a frank generalization which, like those classic logical self-contradictors, contains the grounds of its own Gogolian undoing. It may well be that both statements are true in this sense: that in speaking of himself Gogol could never be sure that he was lying — or telling the truth. He "confessed" to Smirnova that his relations with literary friends and *confrères* had always been based on his calculation about how each of them could be useful to him, from which he divined "just what could and could not be said to each"; for a variety of somewhat contradictory reasons he said he had never spoken of his personal plans or of "what related personally to [his] fate" (XII, 433). In short, Gogol's few attempts to speak frankly in his letters were all attempts to speak *about* frankness, and one feels in them the anguished desire of a man bewildered by his own chronic evasions and mimicry to find his "real" voice and discover what it might have to say. Beginning already with the later drafts of *Dead Souls*, Volume One, he assumes the authoritative

---

[10] Helen Muchnic, *An Introduction to Russian Literature* (New York, 1964), 97-101.

tones of the prophet; his last book, *Selected Passages*, is written entirely in that vein with few conscious concessions to the perspectives of artistry. This voice, he thought, was that of his very soul, expressing its noblest concerns, inspired by God. But in the fiasco that followed publication Gogol was forced ruefully to recognize that the devil had tricked him; that he had chosen only the least effective and becoming of that "orchestra of voices" which had produced his best narratives; that indirection and implication were his only effective tools; that he was, however, drawn to stable identity and single truth, condemned to approximations.

"I never created anything through imagination", he said (VIII, 446); but he also complained that Pushkin had failed to perceive that the characters which so depressed him in the first draft of *Dead Souls* were all "caricature and my own invention" (VIII, 294). "I cannot say categorically", he wrote late in his career, "whether the writer's field is my field" (VIII, 438); but he also protested that he had no life outside writing and that it was as necessary for him to write as to breathe. One could make a long list of such contradictions — and it may well be that it is precisely their presence which signals the Gogolian authenticity. It seems likely, in other words, that elusiveness was more than a deliberate tactic with him, that it was as well an essential trait of his being. The motif of evasion, after all, is central in both the life and the work — and Gogol seems to have failed only when he cancelled out the grounds of his genius by trying to evade that fact. Such a perspective from absence, indeed, may allow the most fruitful connection of the life to the work — and of both to the cultural situation in which they took their course. I will return to this point later.

If Gogol had, then, made his identity a work in progress indistinguishable, or at least inseparable, from the completion of his life's work, what about the possibility of conventional biography, descriptive if not interpretative? The experiences of a writer's life, after all, can at least give us clues as to his temperament and the transmutation of consciousness from life into art. Here, too, however, Gogol's case proves refractory and anomalous. Baldly put, Gogol seems to have led an adult life with virtually no experiences in it. He himself referred to it as a life of "non-events".

This must be understood in a special sense. The period from roughly 1830 to 1836 was not only the time when most of his works in virtually all genres were written or conceived; it was the time, as well, of his maximal engagement in the life of Petersburg. He was, often simultaneously, writing stories, plays, lectures, essays, and reviews. He worked as private tutor, lecturer (and later professor) in history; he took lessons in painting at the Academy; he visited theaters and followed the magazines; he cultivated the acquaintance of Pushkin, Zhukovsky, and other leading figures in the literary world. In short, the life (like the works) of these years shows all the signs of having been a sustained series of energetic tentatives in several directions at once — an affair in which constant motion took the place of any of the usual continuities in a man's life, and tended to mask their absence. This is no more than appropriate when a young man is finding himself; what makes the case "Gogolian" is that the conflicting tentatives were not resolved but simply abandoned for a dozen years of European expatriation (punctuated by two disturbing returns to Russia, in 1839–1840 and again in 1841–1842). Since the causes of his decision to flee Russia are unclear, that decision itself can hardly offer a perspective on the events that preceded it — and if we seek illumination of the works from the record of the life, the best we can do here is to register the frequency with which the works show a similar abruptness and apparent discontinuity, taxing our sense of adequate form and clarity of viewpoint.

In any case, from this point on dedication to the work in progress largely drains the personal biography (as opposed to the career) of significant content, manifesting something like that "trope of fictiveness" *(figura fikcii)* which Andrej Belyj saw as underlying *Dead Souls:* the specification of featurelessness, the bodying-forth of an absence. In all those years, as before, no scandals, no duels, no arrests; no wife, no mistresses, no sex — "no firsthand knowledge of all those involuntary relationships created by social, economic and political necessity . . . Some writers have spent their lives in the same place and social milieu; [he] kept constantly moving from one place and one country to another. Some have been extroverts who entered fully into whatever society happened to be available; [his] nature made him avoid human contacts as much as possible. Most writers have at least had the experience of parenthood and its responsibilities; this experience was denied [him]". The words are Auden's, describing D. H. Lawrence — and the conclusion he draws can apply to Gogol's case, too, in the late letters and *Selected Passages:* "It was inevitable, therefore, that when he tried to lay down the law about social and political matters ... he could only be negative [or naive — D. F.] and moralistic because, since his youth, he had had no firsthand experiences upon which concrete and positive suggestions could have been based."[11]

Even financial necessity could not bind him. His income, for example, came only from being a writer — but not exclusively from writing itself. He mentions money fairly frequently in the letters and makes it clear that sales of his works brought in amounts that were insufficient and insufficiently regular. He was often nearly penniless, and made to realize, as he wrote in a letter of the late thirties, that a writer actually could die of hunger. Yet he never became a proletarian, was never forced to those desperate expedients which left so deep a mark on Dostoevsky's life and art. He was guarded from this by a series of subventions from the Tsar and "loans" from admirers of his talent — a situation made possible on the historical side by the fact that the professionalization of letters was only beginning in his time, and on the personal by the fact that he had nothing beyond his talent and a frail body to support.

His only needs were for writing and travel — but even the record of his travels cannot be very usefully related to the writings. He did not visit new places to observe, to describe, or to learn, as Tolstoy was to do; his journeys through Europe were neither a cultural pilgrimage nor a flight from creditors, as they were to be for Dostoevsky; nor was Turgenev's mixed political and sentimental motivation for expatriation in any way paralleled in his own. Gogol seems to have chosen new places to visit for their climate, or the presence of well-recommended doctors and well-born compatriots. The journey itself often counted more than the destination, change of place being a spiritual tonic for him, so that when he left Rome or Naples, Paris or Vienna, Ostend or Baden-Baden, one could almost say that he was not so much abandoning a place as resuming a condition.

Evasion being so prominent a feature of the life (as of the works) both must appear hermetic, unapproachable except in their own enigmatic terms, closed to the application of external norms or data. We have seen how guarded and calculated were most of his voluntary relationships; the crucial involuntary ones — and they

---

[11] W. H. Auden, *The Dyer's Hand and Other Essays* (New York, 1968), 293.

are astonishingly few — seem all to have been with his own divided psyche.[12] He did not come to define himself through being bound in some continuing experiential way to class or politics or place — and if he was a slave to his body, he contrived to be that in the one way that could not further his self-knowledge through experience of another: hypochondria, centering on the digestive system.

He did, to be sure, call his works in their succession the history of his soul — by which he meant, apparently, that they represented his evolving sense of values and of the writer's proper mission; but neither in his retrospective tracings or in his fiction itself is there any suggestion that personal experience is a progress or a process, Even his last and highest aspiration — to wisdom — involved, in his view, no necessary connection with experience:

> He who already possesses intelligence and reason cannot receive wisdom except by praying for it both night and day, entreating it of God day and night, elevating his soul to the mildness of a dove and ordering everything within himself to the utmost purity in order to receive that heavenly guest who shuns dwellings where the spiritual household has not been put in order and where there is not full harmony in everything (VIII, 265).

Not Blake's road of excess and not any road at all will lead to the place of wisdom; one "receives" wisdom as a gift. There seems to be a suggestion that one must merit it, but there is no question of earning it actively through engagement with circumstance and one's fellows.

In light of all this, it is not surprising that the major biographical works in Russian seem to confess defeat by the very qualifications of their titles: two years after Gogol's death, P. A. Kuliš published "An Attempt at a Biography of Gogol" *(Opyt biografii Gogolja)*; revised and expanded, it was published as "Notes on Gogol's Life" *(Zapiski o žizni Gogolja)*. The most ambitious work, in four volumes, is Šenrok's no less tellingly entitled "Materials Toward a Biography of Gogol" *(Materialy dlja biografii Gogolja)*; and the most influential in this century (serving as chief source for Nabokov's work, among others) has been V. V. Veresaev's "Gogol in

---

[12] Cf. Victor Erlich, endorsing the relevance of R. D. Laing's existential psychology: "The view of the human psyche that lays special stress on such dichotomies as the real self versus the false, unauthentic self, and pays special attention to the devices of concealment and impersonation employed by a peculiarly frail ego as protection against the encroachments of feared reality is likely to shed significant light on the strange case of Nikolaj Gogol." (*Gogol* [New Haven and London, 1969], 215.)

Life" *(Gogol' v žizni)* — a massive dossier (or "montage", as the form was called in the twenties and thirties) of uncommented and unreconciled documentary excerpts. One may fill in the gaps with supposition — the most serious such attempt is Močul'skij's brilliant version of Gogol's Spiritual Path *(Duxovnyj put' Gogolja)*; or one can take these documentary collections as a kind of do-it-yourself kit for the construction not of a biography, but of a *context* for the eternally absent life, for that life (to put it positively) which Gogol, despite some recurrent doubts, proclaimed from the late thirties on to be his only one: his writing. In that area and in that area only do we have sufficient material — by definition — for a study of this elusive pilgrim's progress: a study of a career and the pursuit of a vocation. History, moreover, lends such an inquiry a particular sanction, for in working out a model of the writer's calling, quite as much as in the fiction he produced, Gogol turned out to be a pioneer, his improvisations the starting point of a tradition.

Let me try to make plain my purpose in juggling all these impossibilities. Gogol himself, in Chapter 7 of *Dead Souls*, contrasts two approaches — the telescopic and the microscopic; and I would argue that both are necessary for any treatment of his work that aspires to completeness. The second, essentially ahistorical, is a matter of close attention to the texts, with an eye to following his own shifting emphases rather than practicing that kind of selective emphasis which can make of, say, "The Overcoat" a plea for the "little man", a warning against following false gods, or a mere playful performance — all of them warranted by one or another aspect of the story, but none of them adequate to account for its complex totality.

I shall not attempt to use the microscope here; the shortest of his stories would require prohibitive expenditures of time. Instead, let me try to suggest something of what the telescopic approach might contribute toward resolving the Gogol problem. This, as I see it, involves the perspectives of literary history — but of a non-traditional kind, which would avoid the conventional rubrics and catalogues of names to investigate *the literary function* as it existed in a given time. My specific starting point is Boris Ejxenbaum's observation, made forty years ago and never followed up, that "the question which troubled Gogol all his life was ... *how*

TO BE *a* WRITER, and *what it meant to be a writer*".[13] This must be understood as referring to something beyond that personal discovery of vocation which faces any beginning writer; for Gogol, I repeat, the question was nothing less than the *invention* of a vocation.[14]

We tend so readily to associate him with the great age of prose he introduced that it may be worth recalling briefly the nature of the cultural situation he entered, characterized as it was by a sense of absence — and of expectation. Here are some representative voices from that chorus of complaint which begins in the 1820's and persists well into the forties:

"We have neither literature nor books", Pushkin writes in 1824 in a note entitled "On the Causes Impeding the Development of Our Literature". The following year Polevoj, in the first issue of the *Moscow Telegraph*, refers to the Russians as "barely having begun to write and study, children in literature".[15] In 1825, Bestužev concludes from his "Glance at Russian Literature During 1824 and the Beginning of 1825" that the general law of cultural (he calls it natural) development does not apply in Russia: "We have criticism but no literature." Vjazemskij, who had written in 1822 that "we are rich in the names of poets, but poor in creations", found a little later that "judging by the books that are printed in Russia, one must conclude either that we have no literature, or

---

[13] Boris Èjxenbaum, *Moj vremennik* (Leningrad, 1929), 89-90.

[14] "I have had no other guides than myself, and can one alone, without the help of others, perfect oneself?" Gogol asked the question with regard to the lyceum education he was just completing at nineteen years of age in 1828 — but he might well have repeated it twenty years later, when his artistic career was effectively over. Belinsky, in fact, repeated it for him, noting in 1848 that "Gogol had no model and no precursors, either in Russian or foreign literature" (V. G. Belinskij, *Polnoe sobranie sočinenij*, X [Moscow 1956], 293).

[15] For this reason he went on to question the possibility of filling a journal exclusively with Russian works: "Would it not be better, instead of proposing publication of Russian works alone and filling it for the most part with schoolboy prose and poetry, to widen the framework and give the readers not Russian work alone but simply everything of an elegant, pleasing and useful nature that can be found in the domestic, as well as in all the ancient and modern literatures. How much there is of interest that is still unknown to us — the sort of thing that a European absolutely has to know!" (*Moscow Telegraph* 1 [1825], "Letter to N. N."; quoted in N. K. Kozmin, *Očerki iz istorii russkogo romantizma* [Saint Petersburg, 1903], 23).

that we have neither opinions nor character". And Venevitinov, about the same time, was calling the edifice of Russian literature "illusory" [*mnimyj*], and the situation in the literary world "completely negative". In a letter to the editor of the *Moscow Herald* (1828) Pushkin refers to "our infantile literature, which offers no models in any genre", and two years later the fifteen-year-old Lermontov indicates in his notebook what this can mean for a beginning writer: "Our literature is so poor that there is nothing I can appropriate from it." In 1832 Kireevskij declares Russian literature "still a baby which is only beginning to speak purely", while the critic Nadeždin, with grateful wonder, acknowledges a few poetic blooms "amid the general void and barrenness". In 1834 Pushkin returns to his theme of ten years before, projecting an article under the title: "On the Insignificance [*ničtožestve*] of Russian Literature."[16]

The list of such complaints could be easily extended, but to little purpose. All those sad discussions of the lack of a Russian literature to discuss are really about the nonexistence of literature *as an institution* — which argued (according to the prevailing Romantic view) an incompleteness in society, of which the institution was to be an expression. Yet the very complaint was itself a beginning and, taken up by more and more voices, turned finally into a *Kulturkampf* on whose battleground the institution came eventually to be erected.

By about 1830, it was becoming clear that the battleground would be one of prose. This was the medium of competition for a broader reading public; it was also the medium for that principled criticism that might aid in the formation of writer and audience alike. The frequent complaints about the absence of a Russian prose in this period thus referred, not always clearly, to a range of interconnected problems: absence of a mature and flexible instrument,

---

[16] Puškin: "On the Causes ...", *Polnoe sobranie sočinenij v desjati tomax* Izdanie vtoroe (AN SSSR, Moscow, 1956–58), VII, 18; "Letter to the editor ...", *ibid.*, 71; "On the Insignificance ...", *ibid.*, 306. A. A. Bestužev: *Poljarnaja zvezda, izdannaja A. Bestuževym i K. Ryleevym* (Moscow–Leningrad, 1960), 488. Vjazemskij ("We are rich ..."): quoted, along with Venevitinov, in N. K. Kozmin, *N. K. Nadeždin* (St. Petersburg, 1912), 96. Lermontov: *Polnoe sobranie sočinenij*, IV (Leningrad, 1940), 465. Kireevskij: "Obozrenie russkoj literatury za 1831 g.", *Evropeec* 1 (1832), 100. Nadeždin: quoted in Kozmin, *N. K. Nadeždin*, p. 392.

absence of a normative native style, absence of exemplary genres and techniques in fiction — this last finally subsuming the others because of its (potentially, at least) almost unlimited elasticity, European achievements having already legitimized a view of the novel as incorporating nothing less than "epic and drama, lyricism and philosophy, all of poetry in its thousand facets, all one's age from cover to cover".[17]

For such tasks the language of the salons on which Karamzin had based his stylistic reform was clearly too constricting. Yet no other had become established. The majority of Russian writers, Orest Somov declared in 1828, "either wander off the road [sbivaetsja] into the rough fields of the archaic Slavonic-Russian language; or slip and fall on the ruins once heaped together from alien stocks (Gallicisms, Germanisms and so on); or else sink in the base and swampy ground of the coarse, unrefined language of the simple folk".[18] Pushkin had put it plainly in 1824: "Scholarship, politics and philosophy have still not found an expression in Russian; a metaphysical language is absolutely nonexistent among us. Our prose is still so little developed that even in simple correspondence we are obliged to *invent* turns of phrase to convey the most ordinary concepts."[19] The point was echoed repeatedly: "We need", wrote academician Sokolov, "not poets but people who can manage to write correctly and clearly in prose: we have neither an epistolary nor a business style".[20]

Among the reasons for this situation, one of the chief ones clearly had to do with the cosmopolitan eccentricity of the educated classes — with the fact, as Bestužev noted, that "we have been brought up by foreigners, and have drunk in with our mothers' milk non-Russianness *(beznarodnost')* and admiration only for what is foreign". The result was derivativeness: "There was a time when we were misguidedly wont to sign in the manner of Sterne; then we

---

[17] Bestužev (Marlinskij) in the *Moscow Telegraph* (1833); quoted in N. K. Kozmin, *Očerki iz istorii russkogo romantizma. N. A. Polevoj kak vyrazitel' literaturnyx napravlenij sovremennoj emu èpoxi* (St. Petersburg, 1903), 374.
[18] *Severnye cvety za 1829 g.* (St. Petersburg, 1828), 83–84; quoted by V. V. Vinogradov, "Jazyk Gogolja i ego značenie v istorii russkogo jazyka", in V. V. Golubkov and A. N. Dubovikov, eds., *Gogol' v škole* (Moscow, 1954), 58.
[19] "O pričinax, zamedlivšix xod našej slovesnosti", in *Polnoe sobranie sočinenij v desjati tomax* VII (Moscow, 1958), 18.
[20] Quoted in V. V. Vinogradov, *Stil' Puškina* (Moscow, 1941), 516.

took to being amiable in French; now we have flown off into Never-Never land in the German manner. When will we find our proper sphere? When will we write straightforwardly in Russian? God knows."[21] By 1832, when the fiction of Pushkin and Gogol had already begun to appear, Belinsky's first mentor, Professor Nadeždin, could still depict Russian prose as a tower of Babel, "a confusion of all the European idioms that have overgrown in successive layers the wild mass of the undeveloped Russian word".[22] The general condition of Russian prose, described by Bestužev in 1825 as a "steppe, occasionally enlivened by the swift passage of journalistic Bedouins or ponderously moving caravans of translations", was to persist for two decades before a major wave of settlement began.[23]

The burden of all this complaint was as we have noted, as much cultural as literary: what all these observers missed was a Russian national *voice*. What it might utter, no one could guess; all the stress was on instrumentality. Once discovered, the voice would find its roles — would learn how, in Gogol's phrase, to "give us our very selves". Indeed, its authenticity would be proved by its ability, in one way or another, to do just that.

Implicit here is a reconciliation of two practically contrary demands: for a body of original Russian prose that would at the same time attract a broad readership and still satisfy the serious literary standards of that elite which was most vigorous in deploring the current situation. A class conflict thus underlay literary polemics. For while a literary elite, aristocratic in origin, bemoaned the absence of literature, a party of literary "tradesmen" *(torgovcy)* was nonetheless busy discovering and cultivating a large audience, chiefly through the odd-sounding but unprecedentedly successful journal, *The Library for Reading*, founded in 1834 and based, in the words of its editor, Senkovskij, on a cynical notion that "literature" consisted of "works that serve as light and pleasant reading", inclining to the domestic, cultural, and political pieties. In this view, the writer pursued not a calling, but a trade; he was a purveyor of innocuous tidbits to the literate masses.[24]

[21] *Poljarnaja zvezda, izdannaja A. Bestuževym i K. Ryleevym* (Moscow–Leningrad, 1960), 488, 492.
[22] Quoted in N. K. Kozmin, *N. K. Nadeždin* (St. Petersburg, 1912), 392.
[23] *Poljarnaja zvezda*, 493.
[24] "Brambeus i junaja slovesnosť", *Biblioteka dlja čtenija* 3 (1834), 36–37.

If Senkovskij's statement and others like it can be dignified by the name of "theory", it is clear that such theorizing was entirely practical in orientation; its very claim to serious attention rested on the fact of his journal's success in discovering a broad, paying readership. What I would suggest about Gogol is that he be viewed in a like manner — that is, from the practical side. His shifting and elusive theories about art and the artist have received a good deal of attention — at the expense of those writings of his which are addressed to the concrete question of the writer vis-à-vis his public. The latter, seldom referred to and long untranslated, are nonetheless key documents in any understanding of Gogol's career and context.

Of these, the first is his book, *Arabesques* (1835) — a "salad", as he called it in a letter, a mixture of everything under the sun. The book is remembered chiefly for the three famous short stories Gogol included in it; it is on occasion cited for the historical lectures it contains, or such rhetorical-allegorical effusions as those on "Sculpture, Painting and Music", and "Life". In fact, taken as a whole the book appears to be a disguised manifesto, a masked and tentative exploration of problems of effective communication as perceived by a young writer at the time. The censor Nikitenko complained in the same year that Gogol was passing himself off as a universal genius; and indeed what *Arabesques* generally speaking shows is Gogol's attempt to associate himself with a varied company of geniuses by praising precisely what he took to be central in their accomplishment. His role here is that of the intelligent popularizer; and the essays on teaching history and geography amount to an explicit advocacy of the method he has been practicing in many of the other essays.[25] In "A Few Words about Pushkin", the essay around which the whole collection took shape, Gogol confronts directly the problem of the artist and the public. Here he broaches the question of what an authentically Russian poet would be, and, at the same time, indicates the price of authentic innovation, of taking the ordinary, rather than the extraordinary, as artistic subject. The more familiar the object, he writes, the more

---

[25] For evidence of a contemporary recognition of this among students, see V. V. Stasov, "Učilišče Pravovedenija sorok let tomu nazad, 1836–1842 gg.", *Russkaja starina* 2 (1881), 415–416.

one must be a poet in order to draw out of it what is unusual and yet true. Yet such a course, if followed successfully, is "nothing but a miscalculation of the poet — a miscalculation with respect to his multitudinous public, and not with respect to himself" (VIII, 53–54). Gogol's strategy here is complex. By appreciating the high artistry of Pushkin's ostensibly simple pieces, he is validating his credentials to belong, in some sense, in the company of the poet (with whom he clearly identified, and under whose influence, real or imagined, all his major works were conceived). But there is more even than this simultaneous praise and boasting; the article as a whole is also a piece of propaganda, designed to change the thinking of its readers. ("Criticism based on deep intelligence", he writes elsewhere, "possesses a worth equal to that of any original creation"; it makes the critic "even more prominent" than the writer under discussion [VIII, 175].) Addressed to the reading public at large, Gogol's essay suggests a new scale of esthetic values by which conventional public tastes may be sensitized anew. This purely practical intent underlies the pedagogical articles in this collection as well. Gogol in 1835 was concerned with educating an audience.[26]

During this, his Petersburg period, Gogol's most direct practical manifesto was written. It is a long article, entitled "On the Development of Periodical Literature in 1834 and 1835". Threading his way through the intense literary polemics of the day, Gogol refuses to condemn the new "commercialization" of literature, as represented by the *Library for Reading*; recognizing that it indicates a growing demand for literature, especially fiction, he urges rather the responsibility of serious writers to satisfy that demand — in the first place by turning to criticism, by sharing their taste and awareness. The plea is essentially for the deliberate creation of a literary culture, by writers turned critics. European developments should be discussed in print, a usable Russian past should be marshalled, the Russian present should be explained. (Among the key questions Gogol advances for discussion: "Why has poetry been replaced by prose compositions? At what stage of development is the Russian public, and what is the Russian public? In what does

[6] Cf. his letter to his mother of 12 April 1835 where, speaking of literature, he comments: "This is a very difficult art! Do you know that in Petersburg, in all Petersburg, there are perhaps only some five individuals who understand the art deeply and truly ..." (X, 362).

the originality and distinctive nature of our writers consist?" [VIII, 172].)

Summary cannot do justice either to the depth of Gogol's program, or to the shrewd practicality which informs his estimate of the current scene. He had evidently submitted it for publication in the first volume of Pushkin's *Contemporary* in the hope that it would be taken as a program for that journal. It was not — as Gogol recalled eight years later, in a letter explaining his subsequent literary isolation ("The journal had no definite goal even in [Pushkin's] lifetime"; XII, 438). At about the same time, his hyperbolic hopes for a direct effect on a large audience, in the theater, were disappointed by the premiere of *The Inspector General*. "The theater is a great school", he had written, "profound is its allotted task [*naznačenie*]. To a whole crowd, to a thousand people at once, it reads a vivid, useful lesson" (VIII, 562). When that crowd failed to show it had taken the lesson by evidencing on-the-spot moral regeneration — and when critics failed by and large even to discern the lesson — Gogol, a disappointed maximalist, fled abroad to forge in the smithy of his soul the uncreated conscience of his Rus'.

The result was the first volume of *Dead Souls*. Held up by the censorship for an agonizingly long time, threatened not in its "message" but in its artistry,[27] the book finally appeared in 1842 — eliciting a batch of reviews as far off the point as Gogol's own remarks about his book were cloudy. The delays of the censorship Gogol chose to see as a test of people's attitudes toward him (XII, 59). He professed to be uninterested in what the critics had to say — but individual readers were a different matter. Certain that they would take his work up as "an engrossing, diverting novel" and drop it in boredom, he nonetheless put his faith in them. After all, he wrote an unknown correspondent in July, 1842, his works were unlike other works "in that everyone can judge them, all my readers without exception, because the objects are taken from the life that circulates around each one ... I know in advance what

---

[27] See Gogol's letters of early 1842 on official doubts regarding the story of Captain Kopejkin, e.g., XII, 55. *Cf.* Zhukovsky's comment that in Russia laughter was taken as a sign of sinfulness *("U nas smex prinimajut za grex, sledovateľno, vsjakij nasmešnik dolžen byť velikij grešnik")*, N. Barsukov, *Žizn' i trudy M. P. Pogodina*, VIII, 4.

will be printed about me in this journal and that, but the opinions of people who are deeply practical, who know life, who have much experience and much intelligence ... are more precious to me than bookish theories, which I know by heart" (XII, 82).

Here begins the story of Gogol's increasing and quite fantastic attempt to rely directly on his public — with whom, in effect, he proposed what he took to be a mutually advantageous exchange. The public would give him the practical knowledge of Russia he lacked; in return, he would renew the soul and elevate the life of each reader — and so, eventually, of Russia. Queer as the notion of such a bargain may seem, it represents the last stage of Gogol's improvised response to the question of "how to be a writer and what it means to be a writer".

Gogol's sense of responsibility as an author, accepted at Pushkin's urging along with the basic idea for *Dead Souls*, had always pointed two ways: it was a responsibility toward his talent, and also toward his country. By the time the first volume of *Dead Souls* was completed, it was well on the way to becoming obsessive. (Compare the famous passage in Chapter 11, where he speaks of all eyes in Russia as being on him, and asks, "Russia! what wouldst thou of me, then?" — a passage criticized as showing megalomania; to which he protested that though the expression may have been awkward, the sentiment was sincere.) Belinsky had prematurely called Gogol the head of Russian literature in 1835; two years later Pushkin was dead, and if such a titular office existed, it was clear that Gogol had first claim to it. In 1842 his novel confirmed the fact; Belinsky wrote him privately that he was the sole current hope of Russian literature, and called him publicly "the chief poetic talent" on the contemporary scene.[28]

In this situation, it is important to note that Gogol's isolation was not only geographical; the lack of competitors was also a lack of colleagues — an isolation unthinkable already by the end of the next decade, when Turgenev, Dostoevsky, Tolstoy, Goncharov, Saltykov (to mention only the leading figures) had each other to be conscious of — along with a reading public whose tastes and awareness existed in response precisely to that same, shared, pub-

---

[28] In the letter, of 20 April 1842, Belinsky writes: "You are now THE ONLY ONE among us — and my moral existence, my love for creative work is closely bound up with your fate; without you, it would be goodbye for me to the present and future of the artistic life of my homeland."

lic, cultural consciousness, mediated by a criticism which was itself a cultural force.

Gogol, lacking all this, could only turn directly to his reader. This he did publicly in the astonishing preface to the second edition of *Dead Souls*, published, after the original edition of 2,400 had finally sold out, in 1846. It begins: "Whoever you may be, my reader, in whatever place, in whatever calling you may find yourself, whether you are distinguished by the highest rank or are a man of the simple class, if God has granted you literacy and if my book has already come into your hands, I ask you to help me" (VI, 587). The request is for comments, corrections, anecdotes, reminiscences of any kind. Whether one takes this at fact value or accepts Gogol's later allegations of a more devious intent, the fact remains that this is an appeal for help in the form of "statistics" *(i.e.,* facts) about the particularities of a Russian life Gogol had taken as his subject without ever having experienced. "I cannot", he explained, "produce the last volumes of my work until, in some degree, I know Russian life in all its aspects, at least to the extent that I need to know it for my work" (VI, 589).

What Gogol conceived as his side of the bargain was delivered virtually simultaneously with his preface: his famous and ill-fated hortatory hodgepodge, *Selected Passages from Correspondence with Friends*. ("Half of literate Russia", he thought, would read the book.) The most cogent essays are those concerned with writing; rereading them in 1887, Tolstoy singled them out as an excellent statement of "what literature should be", and found "the significance of the writer in general ... defined there in a way that cannot be bettered".[29] For present purposes, the most important piece in the book is also the sanest (and longest) — an article he said he had tried unsuccessfully to write at three previous periods of his career, "What, Finally, Is the Essence of Russian Poetry, and in What Its Peculiarity Consists". Here Gogol is responding to his own call of ten years before, in which he urged Russian writers and poets to take up criticism — to identify a tradition, educate a public, to help create, in effect, the missing institution. In what may be the most perceptive and nuanced sketch of its development to date, Gogol demonstrates clearly how outdated are the com-

---

[29] L. N. Tolstoj, *Polnoe sobranie sočinenij* (Jubilejnoe izdanie), t. 26 Moscow, 1936), 874.

plaints of fifteen years before about the nonexistence of a Russian literature. It exists unquestionably — but it has not yet managed "either to teach society, or to express it" (VIII, 403). His conclusion, clear-sighted and non-prescriptive, is that "neither Pushkin nor anyone else should stand as a model for us: different times have already come" (VIII, 407). He closes with a vision of a new literature which, by expressing Russia, will unite Russians in a recognition that they are "really at home . . . and not in a foreign land" (VIII, 409).

Beyond this vision Gogol was not fated to go. As one Russian critic observed later in the century, he was a typical representative of his age, not only in the works he produced, but also in what he strove so long to produce — and could not. His late search for "facts" was vain, because he renounced the very operations by which his genius had earlier turned "facts" (objects, gestures landscapes) into comic art: exaggeration, absurd juxtaposition, cloudy (because shifting) point of view. "Different times have already come": he was right: that extraordinary intuition which had made his earlier writings so extraordinarily apt an expression of an age of expectation still served him — and he foresaw accurately the advent of a mirroring literature, one based on "truth to life". His loneliness was more than personal, and deeper than that which every original artist knows, for it included the awful loneliness of the initiator of a tradition — a tradition that would ignore the nature of his successes to fulfil the program of his failures.

Philip Rahv, in an article of some years ago emphasizing Gogol "as a peculiarly *modern* instance of the literary artist", nonetheless felt obliged to insist that "it is impossible to abstract Gogol from his historical moment".[30] The contradiction, I submit, is only apparent — and the insight is a key one: it suggests the important nature of *correspondences* within the Gogol problem. They functioned, in his own time, to produce a recognition of his greatness — though one based on a misapprehension of his work; and they remain to be pursued today, in the effort to explore the fundamental nature of that work, and of the whole Gogol phenomenon.

The key to Rahv's paradox, for example, is the *correspondence* between Gogol's unique response to his historic situation and that

[30] "Gogol as a Modern Instance", in Donald Davie, ed., *Russian Literature and Modern English Fiction* (Chicago, 1965), 239, 243.

of later artists (all over Europe) to the "modern" situation which is still our own. In both cases we find a concern with the radical *possibility* of literature; his age felt it because it looked forward to an efflorescence, and ours because it looks back to one which seems to have run its course. Thus the more we understand the Gogolian context, the more relevant his case seems to modern experience, for which the problem has arisen again of *how to be a writer, and what it may mean to be a writer.*

The most original and the greatest of Gogol's works — such works as "Ivan Fedorovič Špon'ka and his Auntie", the story of the two Ivans, "The Nose", *The Inspector General*, "The Overcoat", *Dead Souls* — tend in varying degrees to be problematic, not in the realistic sense that they *depict* problems, but in the more "modern" sense that they *constitute* problems. In *The Dehumanization of Art* (for which Gogol might have served as a particularly interesting illustration), Ortega spells out the distinction I want to emphasize: "Not only", he writes, "is grieving and rejoicing at such human destinies as a work of art presents or narrates a very different thing from true artistic pleasure, but preoccupation with the human content of the work is in principle incompatible with aesthetic enjoyment proper". "Artistic forms proper" he observes, " — figments, fantasy — are tolerated only if they do not interfere with the perception of human forms and fates. As soon as purely aesthetic elements predominate and the story of John and Mary grows elusive, most people feel at a loss what to make of the scene, the book, or the painting."[31]

Compare the ending of "The Nose", a story that tells of the mysterious loss and no less mysterious recovery of a self-important official's olfactory organ — which uses its brief freedom to impersonate a State Councillor. On the last page the narrator steps forward to acknowledge a few of the improbabilities of his tale, and to observe, for and with his reader: "But what is strangest of all, what is most incomprehensible, is that authors can take up such subjects. I confess, that is completely unfathomable, it's like . . . no, no, I can't understand it at all . . ." The artifice of the literary work could hardly be proclaimed more openly. Comparable examples abound in the works I have mentioned.

[31] Jose Ortega y Gasset, *The Dehumanization of Art and Other Writings on Art and Culture* (Garden City, 1956), 9.

Gogol asserts in Chapter 7 of *Dead Souls* that "a great deal of spiritual depth is required to throw light upon a picture taken from a despised stratum of life, and to exalt it into a pearl of creation". Elsewhere he repeats the phrase; it is one of his favorites. "Pearl of creation": he could not have found an apter image for his own practice. For like pearls, his works were produced and polished by a process of gradual accretion and embellishment, their starting point often the most minimal situation "from a despised stratum of life". His characters do not develop; they are progressively revealed through the addition of another and yet another translucent, nacreous layer.

These layers are verbal. Words which seem to represent things in fact do more; they transmute them. The word, Gogol said, is "God's highest gift to man". "One marvels at how precious our language is: *every sound* is a gift; everything is grainy, tangible *(krupno)*, like the pearl itself, and indeed *it may happen that the name is even more precious than the thing itself.*"(VIII, 279). Thus his notebooks abound not in observations or situations, but in lists of words, names of objects or activities or people, whose attraction lay in some arresting power of association or simple sonority.

His gift was for combining them. Rozanov noted what Belyj was later to analyze. Claiming a profound subversive effect for the story of Captain Kopejkin, which he said robbed the war with Napoleon of all its authentic grandeur — and that without any sneering or scoffing — he explains: these are "pages like other pages. Only the words are somehow set up in a special way [*Tol'ko kak-to slovečki postavleny osobenno*]. How they are set up is a secret known to Gogol alone. For him words [*slovečki*] were some sort of immortal spirits; somehow each little word knew how to say what it had to, and do what it had to. And once it's gotten inside the reader's skull, you can't get that word out with steel pincers."[32]

This skill — as George Ivask has observed — is shared by most of the vulgarians — *pošljaki* — who populate his pages, their "human" insignificance redeemed by the fact that they are great wordsmiths [*velikie slovesniki*]. Language, concrete and seemingly familiar, but presented in astonishing and unprecedented combina-

---

[32] Quoted in V. V. Veresaev, *Kak rabotal Gogol'* (Moscow, 1934), 76.

tions, *is* the real hero of his works; and the range of possibility he discovered has yet to be exhausted by his successors.[33]

Thus the phrase which Šestov applied to Chekhov's work — "creation out of nothing" — seems in fact much more applicable to Gogol's. The reader who looks to him for lessons learned or illustrated, for experiential value of some kind, is bound to be baffled. For Gogol's most memorable characters seldom aspire, achieve, change, or learn. Their stories as such are, as Gogol himself recognized, exhibitions; they are also, as Boris Ejxenbaum pointed out, performances. And it is in the brilliance of the narrative performance, in the management of those grainy words, so much more valuable than the things they designate, that we in fact find a peculiar problematics. Just as it is there, if anywhere, that we must pursue the question of the sense or import of each work.

We struggle not to *understand* but simply to picture Major Kovalev's nose as it reprimands him with a frown in the Kazan Cathedral; in the same way we struggle to picture Akakij Akakievič — and cannot get past the obtrusive syntax: "a clerk of whom it could not be said that he was very remarkable, shortish in height, rather pockmarkedish, rather reddish-haired, rather even purblindish to look at, with a small bald spot on his forehead [!], with wrinkles along both sides of his cheeks [!], and a face of the color that is called hemorrhoidal."

Gogol himself, in short, supplies the temptation to speak of his words as if they referred to nothing outside themselves; that is, to no system outside their own. They do, of course, have external referents; and they do "say something" about the Russia of his time. But not directly. If Nabokov is wrong to deny any important connection with what Russians so confidently refer to as "reality", he errs no more than Belinsky did in finding Gogol's representation of that reality faithful in every particular.

Here again the concept of correspondences can be of use.

---

[33] The point is made in a suggestive article by Jurij Ivask, "Literaturnye zametki", *Mosty* 6 (1968), 171–180. Cf. Victor Erlich's admirable formulation: "In this lifeless, stagnant universe, language is the only active protagonist, the only dynamic force, both as a great impersonator of dismal reality and as a major avenue of escape from it". (*Gogol* [New Haven and London, 1969], 221).

Form and content, often hard to distinguish clearly, show in Gogol's work a particular tendency to merge; which is to say that *theme* and *technique* become quite inextricably fused. The technique is not simply the best way to express a theme; it is the *only* way. Consider the ending of *Dead Souls*, where Čičikov's carriage abruptly yields place to another, which soars away into the distance:

> And art thou not, too, Russia, soaring along like a nimble troika that is not to be overtaken? The road smokes under thee, the bridges thunder, everything falls back and remains behind ... Russia! Whither then art thou rushing? Give answer. It gives no answer. The bell pours out a wondrous ringing; the air, torn to pieces, thunders and becomes wind. Everything on earth flies past and, gazing askance, all other peoples and nations stand aside and yield the right of way.

The technique here is evasion — but now openly expressed as theme. Moreover, the technique, which has been to emphasize meaninglessness and absurdity, turns that emphasis around in this closing passage with a rhetorical question that promises an answer, and a *sense*, in the future ...

From this nexus, the correspondences go in two directions: toward Gogol as creator, and toward the effect of his creation on his contemporary audience. The thematic cluster here — which could be matter for a separate essay — is perhaps the central one in Gogol: *road/evasion/metamorphosis.*

In his letters, Gogol continually stresses the special importance which the road had for him personally. "I absolutely need the road." "I am counting heavily on the road." M. Cabanès, in his book *Grands névropathes*, sees this as "the blood of the Cossacks, of the wandering adventurer", showing itself in "sudden burst[s] of atavism".[34] Gogol knew better. "The road", he said, "is my only medicine". "The road saved me." "My creative capacity is only too connected with this [sudden need to travel]" — "a need which I cannot explain to myself", but on which his health, "spiritual and physical", depended. The urge to flight may have meant different things at different times — flight from himself (Gogol), or from "his own vision of things" (Belyj) — but the common impulse was towards freedom from fixity, definition, accountability.[35]

---

[34] Auguste Cabanès, *Grands névropathes* III (Paris, 1935), 248.
[35] XI, 315, 319, 325; XII, 29; X, 148; Andrej Belyj, *Masterstvo Gogolja* (Moscow–Leningrad, 1934), 181.

This theme recurs in a great many of the works, and gives a number of them their endings: the two Ivans, "The Portrait", "Diary of a Madman", *Marriage* (where Podkolesin jumps out a window), *The Inspector General* (where Xlestakov, "a phantasmagoric figure . . . like a false, personified deception, is carried away together with the troika God knows where" [IV, 118]) — and, as we have seen, *Dead Souls*.

But the road functions in yet another way for Gogol: as *cultural metaphor*. In *Dead Souls*: "What tortuous, out-of-the-way, narrow, impassible *roads*, leading far off to the side, has mankind chosen for itself in its aspiration to achieve eternal truth . . ." How many times, he exclaims, has it followed will-of-the-wisps up to the very edge of the abyss, "only to ask each other then with horror: 'Where is the way out, *where is the road?*'" (VI, 210–211). His sense of the cultural situation in the late forties was expressed in the notion that "the world is on the move [literally, on the road], and not at a resting place" [*mir v doroge, a ne u pristani*] (VIII, 455).

The terms are astonishingly vague — and seem to reflect accurately Gogol's very uncertain *knowledge* of the Russian scene. Indeed, Vengerov created something of a scandal in 1913 when he published an article entitled, "Gogol Absolutely Did Not Know Real Russian Life" [*Gogol' soveršenno ne znal real'noj russkoj žizni*], in which he demonstrated that the author of *Dead Souls* had spent a total of only forty-nine days in the Russian provinces, most of them inside a carriage ![36]

This was scandalous because most readers continued to assert, with Herzen and Belinsky, that Gogol had given a faithful depiction of provincial life — when in fact what he was doing was evading lifelike proportions and clarity of statement to body forth an emptiness, a collection of illusions, at best a virtuality. And the very resourcefulness of the bodying-forth turned out to have the greatest possible public validity. His ignorance of Russia, his lack of personal experience, his avoidance of the unsolved problems of literary form — all turned out to be positive. Because the brilliance of his linguistic performance and the sureness of his symbolic intuitions *made manifest and palpable* the absences so many of the intelligentsia were deploring — and so, in a sense, destroyed

---

[36] S. A. Vengerov, *Pisatel'-graždanin. Gogol'* (Saint Petersburg, 1913).

them, turned them into a paradoxical presence, capable of provoking further developments.[37]

Belyj put it well: if Russian prose literature — which subsumed so much of intellectual life in the nineteenth century — began with Pushkin, it took off with Gogol. His work was more hailed than examined in his own time — which is understandable. And it offered the grounds for its own speedy supersession — by a new generation of writers who would deal with the problems he could only foresee, subordinating his lyricism and irony to the investigation of experience, and elaborating in practice the model of the Russian writer which he could only proclaim. (There is another set of correspondences to be worked out in this connection — but that is matter for another occasion.)

What I have tried to suggest in these fragmentary remarks is that there is an alternative to asking the usual (and usually unanswerable) questions about Gogol: what did he read? was he a realist or a symbolist? what was his illness? how genuinely religious was he? and so on. Specifically, my suggestion is that if we seek instead to identify all the constituent elements of the Gogol problem *as such* — historical and stylistic, contextual and immanent, absences and presences — the patterns they reveal may go far toward constituting an answer to the riddle of his existence, in the past as in the present.

Harvard University

---

[37] See D. N. Ovsjaniko-Kulikovskij, "Gogol' i ljudi sorokovyx godov", in his *Istorija russkoj intelligencii*, I (Moscow, 1908), for a perceptive discussion of this problem.

CATHEDRAL FOLK: APOTHEOSIS OF ORTHODOXY OR ITS DOOMSDAY BOOK?

HUGH McLEAN

In the years 1866–1872, while he was writing *Cathedral Folk* and its various antecedents, Leskov was intermittently aware that he had undertaken something far more lasting and significant than his "anti-nihilist" novels. However passionate he felt, at the time he wrote them, about *No Way Out*, *The By-passed*, and later *At Daggers Drawn*, and however convinced he was of their historical truth and moral rightness, at bottom Leskov knew perfectly well that they were not major works of art. They were, as he said of *No Way Out*, "hasty, journalistic jobs".[1] Yet he, too, like all his contemporaries, was deeply influenced by two characteristic mid-nineteenth-century notions — or perhaps we would prefer to call them prejudices — which led him to expend so much effort for such meagre artistic results. These were, first, the "ideology prejudice", still rampant in the Soviet Union, according to which the most important thing about a work of literature is not its artistic quality, but its political or philosophical "line"; and second, the "size prejudice", according to which sheer bulk is regarded as a measure of artistic importance and seriousness. All his life and even to this day Leskov's reputation has suffered from this latter idea. A writer is to be judged by his "major efforts", i.e., his longest and most substantial works. In Leskov's case this meant his big novels; these novels were obviously second-rate; and therefore Leskov could be safely pigeon-holed as a second-rate, minor writer, "very close to Mel'nikov and on a level with Avdeev", as one critic put it as late as 1891 — an absurd misestimate typical of the period.[2] Leskov

---

[1] [N. S. Leskov], "Ob"jasnenie g. Stebnickogo", *Biblioteka dlja čtenija* 12 (December, 1864), 1.

[2] M. A. Protopopov, "Bol'noj talant", *Russkaja mysl'* 12 (December, 1891), 265. Pavel Mel'nikov (1819–1883), Leskov's "tutor" in matters regarding the Old Believers, was the author of bulky "ethnographic" novels (written

might be credited with a few pretty good short stories, but no one could buy his way to top artistic rank with such small change.

Yet there was one work that was different, one that could not be written off as another *No Way Out* or *At Daggers Drawn*. It was bulky enough to qualify as a heavyweight, yet shared the artistic quality of "Lady Macbeth" or "The Battle-axe". That work, of couse, was *Cathedral Folk*. *Cathedral Folk* is probably the only one of Leskov's LONG works that on its own merits can be ranked as an indisputable classic. For that very reason, it has perhaps been rated even higher by Leskov's friends and defenders than it deserves. Especially in an age dominated by giant novels, it was comforting for Leskov's advocates, and for Leskov himself, to have at least one large success to point to, one universally acknowledged big monument with which its author's name could be linked as a kind of appellative: Leskov, the author of *Cathedral Folk*, that "magnificent book", as Maksim Gor'kij called it.[3] But now, with the perspective of a century of time and the fact of several lofty reputations, such as Maupassant's or Chekhov's, resting on short stories rather than novels, we may find ourselves, as Leskovian advocates, able to do our author full honors without pinning them all on *Cathedral Folk*. And we may even be willing to concede that this novel does not quite rank among Leskov's very best works.

---

under the pseudonym Andrej Pečerskij) which try to get the maximum artistic mileage out of Russian *couleur locale*. The best known are *In the Woods (V lesax*, 1871–1875) and *On the Mountains (Na gorax*, 1875–1881). Although still remembered, reprinted, and read, Mel'nikov is hardly a major light among the Russian literary luminaries of the nineteenth century. Mixail Avdeev (1821–1876) is a now almost totally forgotten novelist and critic who made an ephemeral splash in 1860 with a novel called *Underwater Stone (Podvodnyj kamen')*, which dealt daringly with the titillating topic of free love.

[3] In his introduction to Leskov's *Izbrannye proizvedenija* I (only volume published; Berlin, 1923), 9. Gor'kij's admiration for Leskov has naturally been the subject of several Soviet scholarly efforts; and Gor'kij's endorsement has frequently been used — not always successfully — as a kind of lever to push the dubiously reactionary and religious Leskov through the Soviet censorship. See, among others, B. M. Drugov, "A. M. Gor'kij o Leskove", *Literaturnaja učeba* 6 (June, 1941), 21–43; L. P. Grossman, *N. S. Leskov* (Moscow, 1945); D. K. Muratova, "Gor'kij i Leskov", *Voprosy izučenija russkoj literatury XI–XX vekov* (Moscow–Leningrad, 1958), 253–259; and N. S. Pleščunov, *Romany Leskova "Nekuda" i "Soborjane"* (Baku, 1963).

However that may be, *Cathedral Folk* is indisputably a big book, and it is certainly a good, if not a great, one. The author had ample reason to regard it with special fondness. "I love my *Dwellers in God's House* so much that I am ready to fuss over them again and again", he wrote in 1871, undiscouraged by the many trials he had undergone in trying to get the book published. "For the sake of your love of art and the idea of art, bestow your love on my *Dwellers* and take care of them. I place my greatest hopes in them."[4] Much later, when translations of *Cathedral Folk* began to appear in Western languages, Leskov felt confirmed in his special affection for this foremost among his offspring. "Axilla is opening for me the doors into European literature", he wrote in 1886.[5] Leskov continued to take pride in the artistic quality of *Cathedral Folk* long after he had repudiated, as we shall see, its ideology.

There is another, extra-literary and cognitive reason for the popularity of *Cathedral Folk*. It is one of the few works in all Russian literature that deals seriously, and from an insider's point of view, with the Orthodox Church — an institution obviously crucial in the nation's spiritual culture, but strangely neglected by its writers. Received as it was with great applause and gratitude in ecclesiastical circles, *Cathedral Folk* has come to be regarded as in some sense the apotheosis in Russian literature of the Orthodox clergy, that forgotten class, so much despised and so little understood by the atheistic intellectuals of the capitals. Revile and scorn it as the intellectuals might, the Orthodox Church was nevertheless historically the most authentic cultural voice of the Russian people, the repository of its aspirations, its ideals, and its art. If you wanted to comprehend the soul of Russia, you had first to understand its religious life.

The chief representatives and spokesmen of Orthodoxy in *Cathedral Folk* are, of course, that contrasting but wonderfully integrated trio of "dwellers" in the Old Town cathedral: Father Savelij Tuberozov, the thoughtful and courageous, if sometimes bull-headed,

---

[4] Letters to P. K. Ščebal'skij of June 8 and October 7, 1871, in N. S. Leskov, *Sobranie sočinenij*, ed. V. G. Bazanov and others (Moscow, 1956–1958), X, 329; 335. (Hereafter references to this edition are given by volume and page number only.) *Dwellers in God's House (Božedomy)* was the title of an early version of *Cathedral Folk (Soborjane)*, partly published in *Literaturnaja biblioteka* 1 and 2 (January–February, 1868).

[5] Letter to S. N. Šubinskij of June 17, 1886 (XI, 320).

archpriest; Zaxarija Benefaktov, Tuberozov's subordinate, the very concentrated essence of gentleness and self-abnegation; and most picturesque, if not most admirable of all, Deacon Axilla Desnicyn, a kind of living oxymoron, the "Cossack in a cassock", a man of giant physique and enormous strength, born to ride the steppes like a warrior of old, doing battle with his Tsar's enemies, who finds himself incongrously clad in a clerical gown and living in the prosaic, small-spirited, and over-civilized nineteenth century.

The first among this trio of divines, and the principal protagonist of *Cathedral Folk*, is Savelij Tuberozov. With respect to Father Zaxarija and Axilla, an element of condescension, and, in Axilla's case, of benevolent amusement as well, is built into our attitude as Leskov manipulates it: they are not our equals. But toward Savelij condescension is hardly possible. It must be realized that for a Russian reader of that time, i.e., a member of the nineteenth-century Russian cultural elite, to view an Orthodox priest as an equal demanded a real spiritual revolution. Two conventional attitudes toward the clergy were possible: condescending benevolence if you were a believer, or contemptuous hostility if you were not; but equality — hardly. Even educated Russians who took their religion seriously and revered their priests as instruments of God still found it hard to respect them as men. And indeed they seldom deserved respect: it was only too true that the average Russian village or even town priest was abysmally ignorant, poor, obsequious toward the gentry, grasping toward his peasant parishioners, dirty, unkempt, and frequently addicted to drink.

But such a typical *pop*, beaten down, over-humble, and mindless, would hardly do as the protagonist of a long novel apparently designed to show the living spirit of Christianity still burning bright in Russian Orthodoxy. Leskov was therefore obliged to create a figure admittedly idealized and atypical: a priest such as he would like all Russian priests to be, intelligent, well-read, thoughtful, warm-hearted, and courageous in his pursuit of truth and righteousness. Such is Savelij Tuberozov. The danger in any such idealization, of course, is that the resulting character may turn out to be neither believable ("Who ever heard of a priest like that?") or even attractive — virtuous characters in literature have an almost irresistible tendency to turn into unbearable prigs. But in Savelij Tuberozov Leskov successfully wrought the miracle: his idealized priest is on the whole both believable and likeable.

One of Leskov's most important techniques for internalizing our view of Tuberozov is the inclusion of his diary, or "Demicoton Book", which occupies a large portion of the first half of the novel. This diary has been greatly admired, both in Leskov's day and later, and it certainly is a stylistic *tour de force*, the very quintessence of a priest's Russian, with its dense concentration of archaisms, Slavonicisms, ecclesiasticisms, and Scriptural quotations. For all its stylistic virtuosity, however, I do feel that this diary is partly flawed by a kind of Victorian sentimentality to which we are somehow less tolerant than our great-grandfathers were. (That doesn't mean we're better; only that we have other ways of deluding ourselves.) However, I am not going to analyze either the style or the sentimentality here.

From the point of view of our understanding of Orthodoxy, an additional disappointment in Tuberozov's diary is the limited view it gives us of the priest's inner life, and his religious life in particular. Neither in the intimacy of the diary, nor at any other point in the novel, do we really see Father Tuberozov, either as man or as priest, in direct relations with his God. We see his Christianity and his Church only as a social, human institution, as a moral force among men in this world, not as a means of contact with the next. The "real presence" of none of the Orthodox deities — God the Father, Jesus, the Holy Ghost, the Virgin, the saints — is felt in the book; and the characters hardly undergo any religious, as distinct from ethical, experiences. Although we learn a greal deal about Father Tuberozov's view of the Church and his program for its reform — his ecclesiastical sociology, so to speak — we find out nothing about his theology or metaphysics. Nor do we ever see him, even externally, in his magic sacerdotal roles — not at the supreme moment in the Eucharist when the apostolic power he wields transforms humble bread and wine into the Body and Blood of Christ, nor, for that matter, at any other moment in the liturgy. Nor do we ever see him in the Confessional, exercising the awesome power vested in him to absolve men of their sins.

Instead, our most powerful impression of Savelij in the Church is his performance as a *preacher*, delivering sermons that burn the hearts of men, until the hierarchy seals his lips. Thus to treat the sermon as the pastor's central religious act is, of course, essentially a Protestant, not an Orthodox position, the more so since Tuberozov's sermons are focussed on moral issues facing his parishioners in this world, not on their relations with God. However praiseworthy such sermons may be, they cannot be regarded, from an Orthodox point of view, as a fulfillment of a priest's most basic function. For in Orthodoxy, as in Roman Catholicism, the *most* vital mission of the Church, and of the priest within it, is not to seek the amelioration of this sinful world, but to save souls. And while salvation always rests as a discretionary power, so to speak, in the hands of God, He has granted His Church certain means to promote that salvation, to increase its probability. Chief among these means are the Sacraments. And of Sacraments there is scarcely a mention in all of *Cathedral Folk*. Indeed, in this ostensibly ultra-Orthodox novel, the author in fact exhibits some markedly un-Orthodox, inherently Protestant ideas and attitudes.

In view of this latent Protestantism lurking in the very heart of *Cathedral Folk*, it will seem less surprising, less startlingly inconsistent to find its author, only three years after its publication, repudiating this book and the Church which it had idealized.[6] The germ of the repudiation was already present in the idealization. In fact, Leskov's allegiance to Orthodoxy was always a qualified one. A letter of 1871, written in direct connection with *Cathedral Folk*, contains the most forthright statement of personal allegiance to the Church Leskov ever wrote:

I am not an enemy of the Church, but her friend, or rather I am her humble and devoted son and a convinced Orthodox — I do not wish to vilify her; I wish her honorable progress out of the stagnation into which she has fallen, crushed by her involvement with the State.[7]

---

[6] In a letter to his friend Ščebal'skij during this trip to Europe in 1875 (July 29/August 10), Leskov wrote: "I will say only one thing, that if I had read everything on this subject [religion] that I have read now, and heard everything I have heard, I would not have written *Cathedral Folk* as it is written ... I do have, however, a hankering to write about a Russian heretic — an intelligent, well read, and freethinking *spiritual Christian*, who has passed through all sorts of hesitations in his search for Christ's truth and has found it only in his own soul. I would call such a story "Fornosov the Heretic", and I would publish it ... Where would I publish it?" (X, 412). There is an illuminating discussion of Leskov's readings and religious crisis in William B. Edgerton, "Leskov's Trip Abroad in 1875", *Indiana Slavic Studies* IV (Bloomington, 1967), 88–99.
[7] Letter to P. K. Ščebal'skij of June 8, 1871 (X, 329).

Yet if we examine this statement closely, its negative features stand out far more than its positive ones. Not only does it begin significantly, not with an assertion of devotion, but with a denial of enmity, but the whole tone is rather critical and condescending. The Church is judged as a kind of fallen woman, locked in the sinful embrace of the state and sunk in the slough of stagnation. This Church's son may be devoted, but he is hardly humble and certainly not blind to her faults.[8]

Essentially the view of the Orthodox Church Leskov presents in *Cathedral Folk* is that of a sympathetic Protestant outsider: an outsider who repudiates entirely that Church's own conception of its most crucial mission (the promotion of salvation through sacraments), but tactfully refrains from dwelling on this disagreement. Largely ignoring the whole question of the Church in eternity, the Church as a vital intermediary between man and God, Leskov instead concentrates on the concrete social situation of the Church here below, its strengths and weaknesses, its enemies and its friends in the Russian reality of his time. And the picture he paints of this situation is a stark and gloomy one indeed. He shows us a Church so beset by external enemies and so undermined by its own internal flaws and weaknesses that its chances of mere survival, let alone revival, appear very dark. It now seems strange, in fact, that *Cathedral Folk* should have been so enthusiastically received by the Russian clergy and the Orthodox faithful as a great moral boost to their cause from the side of secular literature.[9] Quite apart from its Protestantism, *Cathedral Folk* reads more like the Doomsday Book of Orthodoxy.

As shown in the novel, there were two principal enemies confronting the Church from without in the mid-nineteenth century. The first was the enemy "from below", irrational but historic, still an enormous barrier to spiritual union between the official Orthodox Church and the whole Russian people, namely, the Old Belief, to which millions of simple Russians remained fanatically devoted.

---

[8] On Leskov's relation to the Church, see the excellent dissertation by Brigitte Macher, "Nikolai Leskovs Verhältnis zur Orthodoxie" (Marburg, 1952).

[9] See, e.g., the long anonymous article, "Naše duxovenstvo po belletrističeskim proizvedenijam", *Pravoslavnoe obozrenie* 1 (January, 1872), 73–105; 304–333. It is devoted entirely to an enthusiastic review of *Soborjane*.

The second was the enemy "from above": the secularism and atheism widespread among the educated classes, an atheism which in its most radical form professed a total rejection of the Church as an outmoded, intellectually stultifying, and socially repressive institution.

Leskov originally planned to demonstrate both these assaults on the Church in his novel, integrating them as fundamental conflicts in his plot. In practice, however, they proved too diverse to bring together satisfactorily. The theme of the Old Belief, which was evidently destined to play a major part in the original "Waiting for the Moving of the Water",[10] is gradually crowded into the background by the more current and, to intellectual readers, much more meaningful subject of atheism. In the novel the schism is relegated to the past, to the early portions of Tuberozov's diary, while the confrontation with atheism is acted out in the "present", i.e., the 1860's.

Despite the withdrawal of emphasis from the Old Belief, Leskov manages very well to demonstrate what he considers the essential moral dilemma of the official Church in relation to the schismatics, and his own strong opposition to official policy. As he points out in the letter quoted above, the central moral fault of the Orthodox Church, its principal source of weakness in all its undertakings — not only its relations with the Old Believers — lay in its unholy alliance with the state. According to the Church, the Old Believers were heretics, their salvation jeopardized by their separation from the apostolic Church; according to the state, they were seditionists and rebels, a source of political danger against whom defensive measures were required. This "defense", of course, meant persecution. And since the Church was itself a state institution, it was easy for the two concepts to become fused, and for the Church to become the agent, or at least a collaborator, in the persecution.

To his credit, Leskov was and remained throughout his life a vehement opponent of religious persecution in any form and in the early parts of Tuberozov's diary he graphically demonstrates the disastrous effects of this official policy. As always, persecution saps the moral strength of the persecutors and intensifies the resistance of the persecuted. As a capable and promising young priest,

---

[10] Another of the early titles of *Soborjane* (a quotation from John 5 : 3). "Čajuščie dviženija vody", *Otečestvennye zapiski* 6, 7, and 8 (March 15–April 15, 1867).

Tuberozov had purposely been sent to Old Town, known as a hotbed of the Old Belief, in order to carry on more vigorously the struggle with the schism. But experience soon teaches Savelij that no "struggle", at least on terms morally acceptable to him, is possible. What the authorities want is for him to keep up a steady stream to headquarters of forceful *donosy*, i.e., for him to "finger" active Old Believers with sufficient damaging details so that they can be prosecuted. What Tuberozov wants is to engage in missionary work, i.e., to endeavor to reconvert the schismatics by the force of reason and moral example. He knows well that the moment he collaborates in any police persecutions, all potential moral influence he might have among the Old Believers will immediately be lost. He refuses to be an informer. The result is a head-on collision between him and his superiors, ecclesiastical and secular; and in the end the power of their authority proves stronger than the will of one man.

First, Tuberozov is forbidden, on pain of demotion or even arrest, to engage in his most cherished missionary project, a series of public discussion meetings with leading Old Believers about their theological and liturgical differences. Similarly, Tuberozov tries to resist the time-honored, but to him morally repugnant, custom according to which, at Easter time, the Orthodox clergy made the rounds of schismatic households and collected "donations" — actually a kind of bribe or tribute which more or less bought the donors immunity from clerical denunciations and persecution. These gifts formed an important part of the Orthodox clergy's annual income; and it was no wonder that the deacon — Axilla's predecessor — was so incensed by Tuberozov's prohibition of the practice that he in turn denounced Savelij to the authorities for secretly abetting the Old Belief, even though Tuberozov had paid the deacon his expected tribute out of his own meager funds.

The climax of the government's — for it is hardly the Church's — campaign against the schismatics is the forcible demolition of their chapel. As the chapel was being pulled down by soldiers, an iron cross from the cupola symbolically came loose and hung on a chain; then, "being enragedly urged by the hooks of the destroyers toward falling",[11] it suddenly broke away and fell on the head of one of the soldiers, killing him. The fact that this soldier proved to be a Jew,

---

[11] *Buduči ostervenenno ponuždaem bagrami razoritelej k padeniju* — a good example of Tuberozov's sacerdotal Russian.

and that the Christian Russian government was thus revealed to be sending Jewish soldiers to pull down schismatic Christian crosses — this anomaly incenses Tuberozov far more than the fate of the unfortunate victim.[12] And the persecution, as was to be expected, arouses sympathy among the Orthodox population for their schismatic brethren and indignation against the government's brutality; likewise, the Old Believers' dedication to their faith is only intensified by their sufferings. They march through the streets of Old Town singing "Pharaoh the tormentor".

Completely immobilized in his missionary efforts by the authorities' rigid insistence on a policy of persecution, Tuberozov eventually gives up any thought of "struggling" with the Old Belief. Gradually he learns to live with it according to the old, traditional patterns, under which persecution is somewhat mitigated, not by any formal relaxation or enlightenment of policy, but by the inefficiency and corruption of the system. At last Tuberozov sinks low enough to participate in the annual collection of Easter tribute. As he rationalizes his surrender, it is no use kicking against the goads.[13] And with Tuberozov's moral collapse, the whole subject of the Old Belief slides out of the novel.[14]

The confrontation between the Church and secular rationalism was, of course, a more potent subject than the Old Belief, not only

[12] The idea of making this soldier a Jew was an afterthought on Leskov's part, added to the 1872 version, perhaps with the aim of pleasing his anti-Semite publisher, Katkov. There is no mention of the soldier's religion either in the *Čajuščie dviženija vody* or the *Božedomy* versions of the diary.

[13] Intimidated by the charge of a student who read this article in manuscript that I was stooping to "gutter language", I cite this phrase (Acts 9 : 5) in the Revised rather than the Authorized version.

[14] In the early drafts of *Božedomy* Leskov invoked directly the figure of Avvakum, the great seventeenth-century leader of the Old Believers and himself a writer with a very "Leskovian" feel for the Russian language. With his indomitable intransigeance and courage in the face of persecution, Avvakum was to be a moral model for Tuberozov, even appearing to him in a vision during Tuberozov's "transfiguration" scene. In the published versions of *Soborjane*, however, all direct references to Avvakum have been eliminated — possibly because of the censorship, either of Katkov or of the government, possibly because the paradox seemed too extreme of an Old Believer providing moral guidance to an Orthodox campaigner against the Old Belief. See I. Z. Serman, "Protopop Avvakum v tvorčestve N. S. Leskova", *Trudy Otdela drevnerusskoj literatury Akademii nauk SSSR* XIV (Moscow-Leningrad, 1958), 404–407.

more interesting in personal terms to the majority of Leskov's readers — for whom Old Believers were almost as remote as Hottentots — but ultimately of much deeper general significance. Under the aspect of eternity, the conflict between official Orthodoxy and the Old Belief was a local, transient, and somewhat technical issue, of little interest outside its social and historical context. But in the conflict of the Church with secularism and atheism, it was not the future of Orthodoxy, but of Christianity itself that was in question. Obviously the crisis of Christianity (and other religions as well) in modern times has resulted not from sectarianism or schism, but from the defection of a large part of the cultural elite. It was partly because of the peculiar intellectual and social weaknesses of their church that the Russians were among the first to perceive this threat in its full dimensions: in the nineteenth century, at least, Orthodoxy had few friends among Russian intellectuals. And in all world literature the crisis of faith is nowhere more powerfully expressed than in the novels of Dostoevsky and Tolstoy.

The same, unfortunately, can hardly be said of the representation of *this* conflict in Leskov's *Cathedral Folk*. He cannot match either the cosmic, metaphysical sweep of his great contemporaries, or their emotional intensity. He shows us no Konstantin Levin or Ivan Karamazov wrestling agonizingly with the "accursed questions" of the existence of God and the moral order of the universe. Instead, this whole great theme, the Armageddon of faith and atheism, is both externalized and trivialized. First of all, there is the typically childish, propagandistic equation of faith with morality. The "good" believers, the clergy and the faithful, are lined up on one side of the moral barricade, and the wicked atheists arrayed on the other. Moreover, the battles that take place across this barricade are mostly reduced to the level of humorous anecdote. Leskov never sees, as Dostoevsky did, that the truly significant battle is not the external struggle in the world between atheists and Christians, but the internal conflict between faith and unfaith in the hearts of individuals who feel attracted and repelled by both. Apart from some rather ludicrous "doubts" acquired by the completely unintellectual Axilla during a trip to Petersburg, of which Tuberozov easily cures him, there is no inner struggle for faith in *Cathedral Folk* at all. Leskov seems afraid of attempting the deeper and more poignant theme, the collision between doubt and faith within the mind of a man of both intelligence and integrity.

Even as a purely external confrontation of forces, the conflict between atheism and faith in *Cathedral Folk* is mostly debased and reduced to absurdity, its intellectual content trivialized. Axilla's war with the schoolteacher Varnava Prepotenskij over a human skeleton forms the main "plot" of the early part of the novel. Prepotenskij wants to use the skeleton for "atheistic" anatomical demonstrations to his students, while Axilla considers its non-burial sacrilegious. As Leskov presents it, this "war" consists essentially of the puerile pranks of naughty adolescents. Yet in essence this is *the* war of the century — the great battle of science and religion, probably the most momentous intellectual conflict of modern times — here reduced to the level of a provincial anecdote. And even in this anecdote, Leskov's attitude is ambiguous. With his jejune obstinacy in defending his skeleton and his sophomoric and malicious insistence on waving it like a red flag in the face of that sleepy provincial town, Prepotenskij is certainly both tactless and silly; but on the other hand, neither Leskov nor his readers could hardly commend or admire the superstitious ignorance and bullying of Axilla. Equally anecdotal and trivial are the "devastating questions" put to poor Father Zaxarija Benefaktov by a mischievous schoolboy at Prepotenskij's prompting, e.g., Since whales are known to have very small gullets, how could Jonah have been swallowed by one? The response of this sweet and gentle old priest is equally unlikely to gain our sympathy. Unable to deal with the question intellectually at all, he denounces the boy to his father for insubordination, and the father duly whips his errant son. However time-honored it may be, particularly in Russia, the whip as the answer to an intellectual argument hardly resolves the conflict in favor of Christianity.

An apparently more formidable enemy of the Church than the juvenile Prepotenskij is the Petersburg atheist and ex-revolutionary Termosesov, the chief villain of the novel. This moral monster, who lacks convictions of any kind, religious, anti-religious, political or otherwise, determines to turn to his own advantage Father Tuberozov's conflicts with the authorities. Although he himself has some sort of revolutionary past, he denounces Tuberozov to the authorities as a seditionist, hoping thereby to gain himself a lucrative position in the secret police. He even succeeds in this, but his greed eventually proves his undoing: he is caught counterfeiting banknotes. (This motif of the police counterfeiter was to be picked up much later in Chekhov's "In the Ravine".) He undertakes the seduction of the naive nihilist matron Bizjuxina solely in order better to manipulate her in his nefarious machinations; and he controls his unfortunate colleague, Prince Bornovolokov, by means of blackmail and intimidation. As these details indicate — and there are many more — Termosesov is a ridiculously overdrawn and completely unconvincing figure, one of Leskov's super-black devils utterly lacking in human semblance. Like some of the characters in *At Daggers Drawn*, he is supposed to illustrate Leskov's latter-day theory that by the end of the sixties the erstwhile nihilists of the beginning of the decade had cast aside their ideological fig-leaves and become out-and-out criminals. Like Termosesov, they were no longer revolutionaries, but simply scoundrels, blackmailers, and thieves. Whatever the validity of this theory, partly inspired by the Nečaev affair and its most important literary repercussion, Dostoevsky's *Devils*, Leskov's Termosesov is merely a comic-strip villain who nearly wrecks the novel by his presence. The Termosesov sections of *Cathedral Folk* are as bad as anything in *At Daggers Drawn*, and they certainly give the lie to the absurd myth that *Cathedral Folk* is a tranquil, art-focussed, and apolitical book, free from the tendentious axe-grinding of the anti-nihilist novels.[15] On the contrary, crude anti-nihilism remains the Achilles heel of *Cathedral Folk*. In any case, a bandit is simply a bandit, and cannot be taken seriously as an ideological opponent of the Church or of anything else.

Perhaps a more serious threat to the Church than the avowed atheism of the radicals was the widespread religious indifferentism of the upper classes generally; and, since the administrative apparatus of the government was staffed with members of this class, the *de facto* indifference to the Church of the civil authorities, whatever the official rhetoric in Petersburg. Tuberozov — and Leskov with him, since he does nothing to correct the impression—tends to externalize this problem as well. He attributes the officials' coolness toward the Church to the fact that many of them were of Polish or Baltic German origin and hence hostile to Orthodoxy as Catholics or Lutherans, not to the widespread indifference toward the Church of the Russian educated classes themselves. Thus the

---

[15] Thomas A. Eekman is eloquent on this point. See "The Genesis of Leskov's *Soborjane*", *California Slavic Studies* II (Berkeley and Los Angeles, 1963), 126.

crucial nineteenth-century problem of the loss of faith by intellectuals or at least their withdrawal from active association with the Church is evaded by Leskov and a paranoid, xenophobic myth substituted. In Leskov's novel, for the purpose of substantiating this myth, the administrative apparatus of this ultra-Russian province is represented as nightmarishly un-Russian, filled with sneering Poles and haughty Germans contemptuous of Russia, her Church, and her people. It was more comfortable to blame the troubles of Orthodoxy on the non-Orthodox minorities than to confront the fact that most educated Russians had ceased to have any but vague and casual contacts with the Church.

Since the authorities are indifferentists, or worse still, Catholics or Lutherans, it is no wonder that Tuberozov's denunciations of atheists are met with indifference or ridicule. (It is worth noting that Tuberozov has no compunctions about using against atheists this weapon, the secret denunciation or *donos*, which he had scorned to employ against the Old Believers.) "They are all like that", Tuberozov is told when he complains about the schoolteacher Prepotenskij. "If we discharge him, the next will be still worse." The "foreign" state bureaucracy is thus shown to be a most unreliable defender of the state Church. Likewise, except for the antique Marfa Andreevna Plodomasova, who dies in 1850, the local gentry, though unimpeachably Russian in blood, have little interest in Church affairs, let alone willingness to fight the bureaucracy on its behalf. Like most social institutions, the Church depended for leadership, and for moral and economic support, on the educated classes generally, and on the state apparatus in particular. Yet both these groups, as Leskov shows them, regarded the Church with either indifference or hostility, at best as an anodyne necessary to the untutored masses. It was not a hopeful situation.

Finally, even at the very top of the social pyramid there was little support to be found, little comfort for the Church. Much to Father Tuberozov's discouragement, a Church-supported temperance campaign is successfully halted by the Minister of Finance, who needs the vodka revenues to balance his budget. Rubles weigh heavier than souls. For an initiative of the Holy Synod to be thus overruled by the Minister of Finance, the assent of the Emperor would obviously be required. Though he naturally cannot say so directly, Leskov leads us to the inescapable conclusion that the Orthodox Tsar himself did not rate Orthodoxy very high on his scale of values.

Thus from the lay public there was little enthusiasm for the Church or impetus for its renovation. And the situation inside the Church, as Leskov and Father Tuberozov saw it, was even more disheartening. Throughout the Church's structure, from bottom to top, there were disastrous weaknesses at every point. The village *pop*, supposed to be a source of moral and spiritual enlightenment for his peasant flock, was first of all so badly educated that he had little light to shed, and secondly so poor that he was not only overwhelmed by the most pressing material cares, but constantly tempted to squeeze his parishioners to the utmost on those occasions, such as baptisms, weddings, and funerals, when they could not dispense with his services. In the peasants' eyes, he thus became another of the many parasitic exploiters robbing them of their substance, and much of the priest's potential moral influence was consequently lost. At the same time, he was surrounded, on the one hand, by the indifference or contempt of the officials and the gentry and, on the other, subjected to an extremely harsh, centralized ecclesiastical bureaucracy in which bribery and corruption were rife. Finally, between this village priest and his bishop there was an enormous social gulf. The bishops, always chosen from the celibate monastic ("black") clergy, not from the married priests, were wont to rule their domains like mitred autocrats, with little spirit of Christian humility or even humanity. This theme of the tyranny and pomposity of the bishops is only touched on in *Cathedral Folk*, left smouldering to flare up seven years later in *Trifles from the Life of Archbishops* (1879).

The core of Father Tuberozov's struggle, and his ultimate *podvig*, his feat of saintly courage and martyrdom, is directed not so much against the Church's external enemies, dangerous as these were, as against this internal rottenness in the Church, this stagnant spirit of timidity, time-serving, and mindless subservience to authority. Tuberozov's reforming zeal comes in two bursts. The first occurs at the beginning of his ministry, when as a vigorous and idealistic young priest he had felt strong and brave enough to challenge the system, to try to lift his Church out of the mire. As we have seen, the system ultimately proves far stronger than Tuberozov's idealism, and his efforts to halt the official persecutions of Old Believers eventually trail off in frustration and defeat. Similarly and symbolically, his most substantial intellectual undertaking, a long memorandum entitled "On the Condition of the Orthodox Clergy and on

Means of Improving the Same for the Good of the Church and the State", which after months of toil he duly submits, with beating heart, to his ecclesiastical superiors, has absolutely no reverberation whatever. There is neither reproof nor commendation — nothing. The treatise into which Savelij had poured his intelligence and his love is simply buried in some bureaucratic file and forgotten.

Many years later, after a lifetime filled with many compromises and accommodations to the system, Tuberozov in his old age rises up once more to do battle as a Christian soldier. He has undergone a kind of transfiguration. Once, while travelling, he takes shelter in the woods during a violent rainstorm and is only a few yards away when a giant oak tree is struck by lightning and felled. This storm scene, incidentally, is described by Leskov with great power and beauty. Tuberozov is not hurt, but the lightning seems to have struck his soul. As he puts it, his life is over and his *vita* begins ("Žizn' uže končilas'; teper' načinaetsja 'žitie'.").

On the next day, which is a solemn state festival — probably the Tsar's birthday — Tuberozov summons all the officials of the town, on pain of denunciation, to appear in church. Before them he delivers a blistering sermon, incredibly bold for a Russian priest, on the text "Give the king thy judgments, O God, and thy righteousness unto the king's son" (Psalm 72). The word "king" appears as "tsar" in both Slavonic and Russian Bibles, and the direct application to Russian conditions is immediately apparent.[16] The gist of the sermon is the prayer that God should hold the Tsar's heart in His hands and protect it, since the Tsar is surrounded by corrupt and un-Christian servants, money-changers who should be driven from the Temple; it ends with the plea that God should not let his holy Russia become a laughing-stock among nations because of the wickedness of its false servants.

Under Russian conditions, for a priest to pass such harsh moral judgments, based on religious premises, on the secular authorities seemed the utmost in subversion. As Termosesov exclaims with delight, it is rebellion, *bunt*. All of a sudden an abyss opens: the Church, far from being a prop to the state and the throne, might become the most powerful revolutionary organization imaginable. Not only did its network cover the nation, but its mythology lived

[16] 71 : 1 in the Orthodox numbering. In Russian, "Bože ! daruj carju Tvoj sud i synu carja Tvoju pravdu".

in the hearts of the people as no political ideology ever did. The sermon falls like a bombshell among the Old Town officialdom, and on the third day Tuberozov is arrested and led off to ecclesiastical confinement. For months and months he and his wife live in sequestration. His friends pull every wire they can, but the authorities are adamant. Finally it is arranged that if Tuberozov will only go to the Governor and apologize, there will be no further consequences of his seditious act, and he will be released. But this Savelij will not do: he exhibits the same stubbornness once displayed by Leskov's father in a somewhat similar situation.[17]

The poor *protopopica*, Savelij's wife, dies, in Babylonian captivity, as it were, and it looks as if Savelij will do the same. But at last his friends devise a legalistically satisfying, if morally dubious formula which is acceptable both to Tuberozov and to the authorities. If he is *ordered* to acknowledge his guilt, he will obediently do so, since he will bear no moral responsibility for what he does under orders! Thus Savelij pens the required apology and is at last released, allowed to go home to die.

Most of Leskov's contemporaries, especially those of the conservative, pro-Orthodox camp to which he then belonged, were seduced by the goodness and attractiveness of Tuberozov and his colleagues. They acclaimed *Cathedral Folk* as the long-awaited artistic embodiment of the preeminent virtues of Orthodoxy over other versions of Christianity, quite disregarding the tremendous bleakness and pessimism of the picture Leskov had drawn of that church and its problems. As one of Leskov's archepiscopal correspondents put it, with characteristic defensive xenophobia, "The two priestly types, Father Savelij and Father Zaxarija, and also the *protopopica*, are so fine and so morally elevated that with them our clergy can take its stand before any enlightened public... Compared with the Catholic clergy, even Axilla is a righteous man and a moral personality."[18]

At least one of Leskov's correspondents, however, was more discerning. He noticed, and complained to Leskov about it, that all

---

[17] The elder Leskov lost his post in the civil service for refusing to make the governor of the province an apology he felt he did not owe.

[18] Letter to Leskov from Paul, Bishop of Kišinev (Petr Lebedev), of September 25, 1872, quoted from notes made by Prof. Pierre Kovalevsky in the early 1930's and later kindly made available to me. The letter is now in the Central'nyj Gosudarstvennyj Arxiv Literatury in Moscow. See V. G.

three good clerics are dead at the end of the novel. There is no *smena*, no successors for them (at least none developed at any length), no new generation of courageous and idealistic young priests to show Orthodoxy the "way out" of its difficulties. Nor was there even a prophetic glimpse into the brighter and better future surely awaiting the much reviled Holy Church. Leskov's reply, part of which has already been quoted ("I am not an enemy of the Church, but her friend"), is a fascinating document, both as an expression of his rather forlorn and unconvincing hopes for the future of Orthodoxy, and as a statement of his principles of "realism", i.e., of faithfulness to the reality he actually knew:

> As for the lack of good people to replace Tuberozov, Zaxarija, Axilla, and Nikolaj Afanasevič, there is nothing to be done about it; and no matter how much I would like to gratify your respected love for good people, I cannot find them in the clergy of the Russian Church at the present turning point. The types I have depicted are conservative types; but what the present Church will produce in its progress, that I do not know and am afraid of making mistakes... A chronicle like *Dwellers in God's House* must be strictly faithful to the truth of the day; and I am indignant at you, my most noble mentor. I wish to leave matters with the statement that the "hour of general renewal has struck for the priest's house of Old Town". [This is a slightly altered, "memory" version of the last sentence of *Cathedral Folk*]. But what sort of renewal of the Church this will be with Dmitrij Tolstoy tied to the cross around its neck, that my artistic instinct does not venture to predict to me, and by making such a demand of me, you, I think, are committing the sin of constricting the freedom of artistic feeling.[19]

In the political in-fighting of the late 1860's, Leskov himself had sometimes committed the same sin, constricting the freedom of his own artistic sensibility and wandering rather far from the "truth of the day", in order, as he thought, to promote the good cause and destroy his enemies. As to the subject of religion, on which he felt and thought more deeply, if with less superficial passion, than about

---

Zimina, "Iz arxiva N. S. Leskov", *Zapiski otdela rukopisej Gosudarstvennoj Ordena Lenina Biblioteki SSSR imeni V. I. Lenina*, vypusk 30 (Moscow, 1968), 209; and William B. Edgerton, "Missing Letters to Leskov: An Unsolved Puzzle", *Slavic Review* 1 (March, 1966), 128.

[19] Letter to P. K. Ščebal'skij of June 8, 1871 (X, 328–329). Count Dmitrij Tolstoj, with whom Leskov later crossed swords many times, in 1871 simultaneously occupied the posts of Minister of Education and Ober-Procuror of the Holy Synod. He was regarded as an extreme reactionary.

politics, Leskov refused to be swayed by the propagandistic needs of his party. In *Cathedral Folk* Leskov still had to strike some final blows on his old political anvil, clanging away once more at the diabolical nihilist rascals. Concerning religion and the Church, however, he told the truth as he saw it; and the artistic truth has a way of remaining clean and alive when the party truths of all ages have settled into the dust of the past.

University of California, Berkeley

THE PROBLEM OF CONTEXT AND SUBTEXT IN THE POETRY OF OSIP MANDEL'ŠTAM

KIRIL TARANOVSKY

On Oct. 22, 1920, Blok wrote in his diary:

Гвоздь вечера — И. Мандельштам, который приехал, побывав во врангелевской тюрьме. Он очень вырос. Сначала невыносимо слушать общегумилевское завывание. Постепенно привыкаешь... Виден артист. Его стихи возникают из снов — очень своеобразных, лежащих в областях искусства только.

It is not completely clear whether Blok's last sentence means that the main concern of Mandel'štam's poetry is art itself, or that art is the main source of his inspiration. Whatever Blok may have meant, both assumptions are true.

Я получил блаженное наследство —
Чужих певцов блуждающие сны;
Свое родство и скучное соседство
Мы презирать заведомо вольны.
И не одно сокровище, быть может,
Минуя внуков, к правнукам уйдет,
И снова скальд *чужую* песню сложит
И как *свою* ее произнесет.[1]

These lines were written by Mandel'štam as early as 1914. In June, 1932, the same idea is repeated as Batjuškov's advice to his fellow-poet:

Что ж, поднимай удивленные брови,
Ты, горожанин и друг горожан, —
Вечные сны, как образчики крови,
Переливай из стакана в стакан.

The idea of pouring eternal dreams from one glass to another is further developed in the poem "K nemeckoj reči", written two months later:

---

[1] "Ja ne slyxal rasskazov Ossiana." The italics in all quotations are mine [K. T.].

> Чужая речь мне будет оболочкой,
> И много прежде, чем я смел родиться,
> Я буквой был, был виноградной строчкой.
> Я книгой был, которая вам снится.

The image of the grape line finds its explanation in the poem dedicated to Batjuškov. It is a metaphor for the genuine freshness of poetry:

> И отвечал мне оплакавший Тасса:
> — Я к величананьям еще не привык;
> Только *стихов виноградное мясо*
> Мне освежило случайно язык.

It should be noted that the metaphor of the grape as poetry was already hinted at in "Grifeľnaja oda" (1923), Mandeľštam's most complicated poem about the creative poetic process: "Plod naryval. Zrel vinograd."[2]

The idea of preexistence of poetry (... prežde čem ja smel roditsja ... ja knigoj byl ...) is expressed on a more abstract level in one of his famous *vos'mistišija* (1934). "Lips" in this poem are, undoubtedly, the "poetic lips" (a favorite image in Mandeľštam's poetry), and the whispering which was born before the lips is poetry itself:

> И Шуберт на воде, и Моцарт в птичьем гаме,
> И Гёте, свищущий на вьющейся тропе,
> И Гамлет, мысливший пугливыми шагами,
> Считали пульс толпы и верили толпе.
> Быть может, прежде губ уже родился шёпот
> И в бездревесности кружилися листы,
> И те, кому мы посвящаем опыт,
> До опыта приобрели черты.[3]

[2] This is a good example of a later context explaining an earlier metaphor.
[3] In the first four lines of the poem music is unified with poetry, as it were, and thus the aim of art in a more general sense is clearly stated: it must follow the mood and aspirations of the people. Such artists as Schubert, Mozart, and Goethe followed this principle in their creative work. In regard to Mandeľštam's own poetry, this idea is expressed with the greatest power in a fragment written in 1931:

> Я больше не ребенок.
>   Ты, могила,
> Не смей учить горбатого — молчи!
> *Я говорю за всех* с такою силой,
> Чтоб нёбо стало небом, чтобы губы
> Потрескались, как розовая глина.

Poetry existed even before humanity became aware of it, — Mandel'štam believes. But there were no poets: there were only joyful presentiments:

Поэзия — плуг, взрывающий время так, что глубинные слои времени, его чернозем оказываются сверху. Но бывают такие эпохи, когда человечество, не довольствуясь сегодняшним днем, тоскуя по глубинным слоям времени, как пахарь, жаждет целины времен...

Часто приходится слышать: это хорошо, но это вчерашний день. А я говорю: вчерашний день еще не родился. Его еще не было по-настоящему. Я хочу снова Овидия, Пушкина, Катулла, и меня не удовлетворяют исторический Овидий, Пушкин, Катулл.

Удивительно, в самом деле, что все возятся с поэтами и никак с ними не развяжутся. Казалось бы — прочел и ладно. Преодолел, как теперь говорят. Ничего подобного. Серебряная труба Катулла:

Ad claras Asiae volemus urbes

мучит и тревожит сильнее, чем любая футуристическая загадка. Этого нет по-русски. Но ведь это д о л ж н о быть по-русски. Я взял латинские стихи потому, что русским читателем они явно воспринимаются, как категория долженствования; императив звучит в них нагляднее. Но это свойство всякой поэзии, поскольку она классична. Она воспринимается как то, что должно быть, а не как то, что уже было.

Итак, ни одного поэта еще не было. Мы свободны от груза воспоминаний. Зато сколько редкостных предчувствий: Пушкин, Овидий, Гомер. Когда любовник в тишине путается в нежных именах и вдруг вспоминает, что это уже было: и слова и волосы, и петух, который прокричал за окном, кричал уже в Овидиевых тристиях, глубокая радость потворенья охватывает его, головокружительная радость:

Словно темную воду, я пью помутившийся воздух,
Время вспахано плугом, и роза землею была.

Так и поэт не боится повторений и легко пьянеет классическим вином.
("Слово и культура", 1921)

The Old Testament and the Apocalypse, Homer and Sappho, Ovid and Tibullus, Dante and Tasso, Racine and Balzac, Dickens

---

Cf. also: "Narodu nužen stix tainstvenno-rodnoj /Čtob ot nego on večno prosypalsja" ("Ja nynče v pautine svetovoj", 1937).

One might ponder Mandel'štam's mentioning Hamlet among great artists. By the image of "frightened steps" Mandel'štam describes Hamlet's behavior as man; he presumably considers him also a poet. Not the poem which he (Hamlet) attempted to write, but all his monologues are thus to be considered high poetry. The fact, however, that they were written by Shakespeare leaves Hamlet in the company of Schubert, Mozart and Goethe — as a metonym for Shakespeare.

and Edgar Allan Poe, Deržavin, Batjuškov, Pushkin, Jazykov, Tjutčev, Lermontov, Fet, Blok, Andrej Belyj, Vjačeslav Ivanov, Gumilev, Axmatova — these are only some of the sources reflected in Mandel'štam's poetry, either as obvious reminiscences or as enciphered subtexts. Needless to say, such reminiscences and even direct quotations acquire a new quality in his work. Mandel'štam was not an imitator. This quality of Mandel'štam's poetry was noted by Benedikt Livšic as early as 1919 (i. e. after *Kamen'* but before *Tristia*):

> Не новых слов ищет поэт, но новых сторон в слове, данном как некая завершенная реальность — какой-то новой, доселе не замеченной нами грани, какого-то ребра, которым слово еще не было к нам обращено. Вот почему не только «старыми» словами орудует поэт: в стихах Мандельштама мы встречаем целые строки из других поэтов; и это не досадная случайность, не бессознательное заимствование, но своеобразный прием поэта, положившего себе целью заставить чужие стихи зазвучать по-иному, по-своему.[4]

Mandel'štam might well have applied to himself what he wrote of the poet Annenskij: "... Innokentij Annenskij uže javljal primer togo, čem dolžen byt' organičeskij poèt: ves' korabl' skoločen iz čužix dosok, no u nego svoja stat'."[5]

A close friend of Mandel'štam, Nikolaj Ivanovič Xardžiev, told me on one occasion the following story. A short time before his last arrest, Mandel'štam visited him and complained that he had nothing to read. Xardžiev then gave him poems by Xlebnikov, a novel by Wells, and several recently published French novels. Mandel'štam looked at this pile of books and said: "What can one make of all of this?" ("Čto iz ètogo vsego možno sdelat'?".)[6]

The assumption that Mandel'štam considered his reading as potential raw material for his own creative work seems to be fairly reasonable. Not only literature, but architecture, painting and music, as well as philosophy, history, and even natural sciences were sources of his inspiration. A young Russian scholar called Mandel'štam in a private letter to me "samyj pereliteraturennyj i perekulturen-

---

[4] "V citadeli revoljucionnogo slova", *Puti tvorčestva* 5 (Xar'kov, 1919). Fragments of this article were reprinted in B. Livšic, *U nočnogo okna* (Moskva, 1970); see p. 185.

[5] "Pis'mo o russkoj poèzii" (1922), *Sobranie sočinenij*, III, 34.

[6] The poet's widow also asserts that Mandel'štam had Xlebnikov's poems in Samatixa, where he was arrested on May 2, 1938. See Nadežda Mandel'štam, *Vtoraja kniga* (Paris, 1972), 107.

nyj [russkij] poèt". Therefore Clarence Brown is essentially right when he attributes to Mandel'štam the following thought: "If you would read me, you must have my culture."[7]

Thus, the investigation of all of Mandel'štam's literary and cultural sources becomes a very important prerequisite for a better understanding and fuller appreciation of his poetry. In other words, if we find a subtitle "Pindaričeskij otryvok" in the first printing of "Našedšij podkovu", it means that we have to read Pindar's odes. And I would like to emphasize that such a reading is fascinating indeed. The reader experiences the genuine joy of recognition, joy of discovery, of which Cvetaeva speaks so persuasively in her memoirs, calling it "nesravnennaja radost' otkrytija v sokrytii".[8]

Sometimes this recognition comes immediately, without further investigation. For example, Mandel'štam's line:

Да будет в старости *печаль моя светла* . . .

contains a simple quotation from Pushkin's famous poem:

На холмах Грузии лежит ночная мгла;
Шумит Арагва предо мною.
Мне грустно и легко; *печаль моя светла;*
Печаль моя полна тобою . . .

The problem is more complicated in the first stanza of the poem "10 janvarja 1934", written immediately after the death of Andrej Belyj:

Меня преследуют две-три случайных фразы —
Весь день твержу: *печаль моя жирна,*
О Боже, как черны и синеглазы
Стрекозы смерти, как лазурь черна.

In this case, a new poetic reminiscence is projected, as it were, over the Pushkinian pattern. It comes from *Slovo o polku Igoreve*: "Pečal' žirna teče sred' zemli ruskyja".[9]

---

[7] "On Reading Mandel'štam", Osip Mandel'štam, *Sobranie sočinenij*, Vol. I 2nd ed.; 1967), XIV.

[8] "Kstati, zametila: lučšie poèty (osobenno nemcy: voobšče — lučšie iz poètov) často, berja èpigraf, ne prostavljajut otkuda, živopisuja — ne prostavljajut — kogo, čtoby pomimo iskonnoj sokrovennosti ljubvi i govorenija vešči samoj za sebja dat' lučšemu čitatelju ètu — po sebe znaju! — nesravnennuju radost': v sokrytii otkrytija" ("Istorija odnogo posvjaščenija", *Oxford Slavonic Papers* XI [1964], 123).

[9] The idiom from *Slovo* was used by Mandel'štam also in his translation (dated January 4–8, 1934; Belyj died on January 8) of the 319th sonnet of

I would like to mention parenthetically that the images of the dragonflies of death and of the black azure have their source in Belyj's symphony *Kubok metelej* (pp. 131–132):

Холодные стрекозы садились на окна и ползали по стеклу... Прыснули вверх снега и как линии качались над домами. Обрывались *стеклянеющими стрекозами*, *стрекозы* садились на окна, смерзались снегом. Стеклянели там *мертвыми* лилиями.

And further (p. 224):

Милое, милое небо сияло — милая, милая *гробная лазурь*.

Moreover, we can find in Belyj's poetry the adjective "black" applied to azure, in his *tanka* "Lazuri" (1916):

Светлы, легки лазури...
Они — черны, без дна;
Там — мировые бури.
Там жизни тишина:
Она, как ночь, черна.[10]

It is not surprising that Mandel'štam, mourning the death of Belyj, recalls the images from his writings.[11]

As we see, the echoes of Pushkin, *Slovo o polku Igoreve*, and of Belyj constitute a SUBTEXT of the stanza just quoted.

It is not always so easy to find a subtext in the poetry of Mandel'štam.

Petrarch ("Promčalis' dni moi...") — "I dí miei piú leggier che nesun cervo"):

О, семицветный мир лживых явлений —
Печаль *жирна* и умиранье наго!

(*Sobranie sočinenij*, Vol. I [2nd ed.; 1967], No. 491)

[10] Mr. Steven Broyde, my student, called my attention to this *tanka*.
[11] In another poem dedicated to the memory of Belyj ("Golubye glaza i gorjaščaja lobnaja kost'") the image of the dragonflies is repeated once more:

Как *стрекозы садятся, не чуя воды, в камыши*,
Налетели на мертвого жирные карандаши.

This image, likewise, recalls a similar one in *Kubok metelej*:

Озеро, заженное искрами, казалось застывшим зеркалом... испод ветром колеблемых *камышей* взлетали *стрекозы* (99)... Вот она скрылась в зеленых *камышах*: там слетела с нее одежда; там *пляшущие стрекозы садились* к ней на плечи и грудь (100)...

At the end of his article "Slovo i kul'tura" (1921), Mandel'štam has the following statement:

Говорят, что причина революции — *голод в межпланетных пространствах*. Нужно рассыпать *пшеницу по эфиру*.[12]

The same image occurs in his poem "A nebo buduščim beremenno" (1923):[13]

> Итак, готовьтесь жить во времени,
> Где нет ни волка, ни тапира,
> А небо будущим беременно,
> *Пшеницей сытого эфира.*

In my Harvard seminar on Mandel'štam (spring 1968) all the participants were puzzled by this image. The verb *govorjat* indicated that it was a quotation. In June of the same year, during my visit to Moscow, I asked Mandel'štam's widow, Nadežda Jakovlevna, whether she knew the source. Her answer was: "He just wrote it,

---

I am also tempted to compare the image of dragonflies in one of Mandel'štam's earliest poems, "Medlitel'nee snežnyj ulej" (1910), with Belyj's "Zima" (1907):

> И, если *в ледяных алмазах*
> Струится вечности *мороз*,
> Здесь — трепетание *стрекоз*
> Быстроживущих, синеглазых.
>
> (Мандельштам)

> Пусть за стеною, в дымке блеклой,
> Сухой, сухой, сухой *мороз*, —
> Слетит веселый рой на стекла
> *Алмазных*, блещущих *стрекоз*.
>
> (Белый)

In both poems dragonflies appear in a cheerful description of winter. In Mandel'štam, the dragonflies are a metaphor for a turquoise-blue veil *(birjuzovaja vual')*; in Belyj, they serve as a metaphor for snowflakes.

[12] "Slovo i kul'tura" was published in the almanac *Drakon* (1921). When Mandel'štam reprinted the essay in his book *O poèzii* (1928), the sentence quoted above was changed: "*Kto skazal*, čto pričina revoljucii — golod v mežduplanetnyx prostranstvax?" This is obviously a rhetorical question: Mandel'štam knew the answer.

[13] This poem was published for the first time in the almanac *Lët* (1923) as a part of the cycle which included two other poems dealing with the theme of aviation: "Veter nam utešen'e prines" (1922) and "Kak tel'ce malen'koe krylyškom" (1923).

and I was always angry with him" ("Èto on prosto tak napisal, i ja vsegda na nego serdilas' "). However, Mandeľštam wrote nothing *prosto tak*. Recently, the subtext has been found by one of the participants of my seminar, Mr. Omry Ronen. The image comes from the mystical philosophy of G. I. Gurdžiev (Gurdjieff), who believed that organic life on the Earth fed the Moon and other celestial bodies, that wars and revolutions were results of planetary influences, particularly — that they were provoked by the hunger of the Moon.[14]

---

[14] Gurdžiev used to promulgate his teaching in circles of his followers in Moscow and Petrograd (1915–1917), and in the Caucasus (Essentuki, Sochi, Tiflis, 1917–1919). In 1919 he even opened the Institute for Harmonious Development of Man in Tiflis. In June, 1920, he left Georgia for Constantinople "with a fairly large company". Mandel'štam could have heard about Gurdžiev's teaching either in Moscow or in Petrograd, but most probably in Tiflis, where he spent the summer and fall of 1920.

Gurdžiev's cosmology was described by P. D. Uspenskij (Ouspensky) in his book *In Search of the Miraculous* (N. Y., 1949). Uspenskij quotes the following statement made by Guržiev at the beginning of World War I (p. 24): "What is war? *It is the result of planetary influences*. Somewhere up there two or three planets have approached too near to each other; tension results... For them it lasts, perhaps, a second or two. But here, on the earth, people begin to slaughter one another, and they go on slaughtering maybe for several years... They fail to realize to what an extent they are mere pawns in the game. They think they signify something; they think they can move about as they like; they think they can decide to do this or that. But in reality all their movements, all their actions, are the result of planetary influences. And they themselves signify literally nothing. Then the moon plays a big part in this. But we will speak about the moon separately". The role of the Moon is explained on p. 57: "The evolution of large masses of humanity is opposed to nature's purposes. The evolution of certain small percentage may be in accord with nature's purposes... There exist, therefore, special forces (of a planetary character) which oppose the evolution of large masses of humanity and keep it at the level it ought to be. For instance, the evolution of humanity beyond a certain point, or, to speak more correctly, above a certain percentage, would be fatal for the *moon*. The moon at present *feeds* on organic life, on humanity. Humanity is a part of organic life; this means that humanity is *food* for the moon. If all men were to become too intelligent they would not want to be eaten by the moon." (See also p. 139.) This "cosmic conflict", according to Gurdžiev, can be solved by the evolution of organic life (p. 305): "Organic life... has to evolve, to adapt itself to the needs of the planets and the earth. Likewise also the moon can be satisfied at one period with the food which is given her by organic life of a certain quality, but afterward the time comes when

Mandeľštam liked to dream about the happy life of humanity, its "golden age", past or future. In 1919, during the height of the civil war, he turned himself to Hesiod's myth of "holy islands".[15] In the early twenties, facing the threat of a new intervention by Western allies, Mandeľštam transformed Gurdžiev's fantastic cosmology into a new poetic myth.

All poets have their favorite themes, their favorite images, and even their favorite words. All these recurrent themes and images form inner cycles in the work of a given poet, cycles which very often cannot be placed within exact chronological limits. Moreover, such recurrent themes and images may be characteristic of several poets, often independent of both the so-called poetic schools and even of historical periods. For example, many Russian poets of the 20th century were fascinated by the image of the ship, including such different poets as Blok, Gumilev, Majakovskij, Mandeľštam, and B. Livšic. An autobiographic image of crucifixion is common to many 20th century Russian poets (Belyj, Brjusov, Blok, Xlebnikov, Majakovskij, Esenin, Pasternak, and others). There are hundreds of Russian poems written in trochaic pentameter which deal with a dynamic theme of the road and a static theme of life. All these poems form a "Lermontovian cycle", as I have called it, which begins with Lermontov's "Vyxožu odin ja na dorogu" and leads to Blok's "Vyxožu ja v puť otkrytyj vzoram", to Majakovskij's "procyganennyj romans" ("Maľčik šel v zakat glaza ustavja"), or to Pasternak's "Gamlet" ("Gul zatix. Ja vyšel na podmostki").[16]

Needless to say, we receive more poetic information when we put a poem in a broader context and reveal its links with other texts.

---

she ceases to be satisfied with the food, cannot grow on it, and begins to get hungry. Organic life must be able to satisfy this hunger, otherwise it does not fulfill its function, does not answer its purpose. This means that in order to answer its purpose organic life must evolve and stand on the level of the needs of the planets, the earth and the moon." — Mandeľštam's *pšenica sytogo èfira* might be compared also to Esenin's *lunnyj xleb* and to his image of cosmic satiation and happiness: "Zakin' ego [mir, šar] v nebo, /Postav' na stolpy!/ Tam *lunnogo xleba*/ Zlatjatsja snopy. //Tam golod i žažda/ V kornjax ne pojut./ No zreet odnaždnyj/ Svet angeľskix jurt." ("Otčar' ", 1917).

[15] See my article "Pčely i osy v poèzii Mandeľštama", *To Honor Roman Jakobson* III (The Hague, 1967), 1985-87.

[16] See my paper "O vzaimootnošenii stixotvornogo ritma i tematiki", *American Contributions to the Fifth International Congress of Slavists* I (The Hague, 1963).

At this point I shall analyze Mandelštam's poem "Koncert na vokzale" (1921) in terms of context and subtext in order to show how this concept works. However, before doing so, I might ask a question: what would Mandelštam himself think about such a method? The answer to this question can be found in his article "Barsuč'ja nora" and in his essay "Razgovor o Dante":

Установление литературного генезиса поэта, его литературных источников, его р о д с т в а и происхождения сразу выводит нас на твердую почву. На вопрос, что хотел сказать поэт, критик может и не ответить, но на вопрос, откуда он пришел, отвечать обязан ...

«Барсучья нора», 1922

Конец четвертой песни «Inferno» — настоящая цитатная оргия. Я нахожу здесь чистую и беспримесную демонстрацию упоминательной клавиатуры Данта.

Клавишная прогулка по всему кругозору античности. Какой-то шопеновский полонез, где рядом выступают вооруженный Цезарь с кровавыми глазами грифа и Демокрит, разъявший материю на атомы.

Цитата не есть выписка. Цитата есть цикада. Неумолкаемость ей свойственна. Вцепившись в воздух, она его не отпускает.

«Разговор о Данте», 1933

Mandelštam was not a poet of large forms; he did not write long poems or novels. But, as a matter of fact, his entire creative work is one entity, one large form: his unique poetic vision of the world, or — in more modern terms — the genuine poetic model of the world, created by him.

Many themes and images occur both in his poetry and in his prose. This is the case with his poem "Koncert na vokzale".

A realistic description of concerts held in Pavlovsk's railroad station may be found in *Šum vremeni*, in the chapter "Muzyka v Pavlovske" (first publication in 1925):

В середине девяностых годов в Павловск, как в некий Элизий, стремился весь Петербург. Свистки паровозов и железнодорожные звонки мешались с патриотической какофонией увертюры двенадцатого года, и особенный запах стоял в огромном вокзале, где царили Чайковский и Рубинштейн. Сыроватый воздух заплесневевших парков, запах гниющих парников и оранжерейных роз и навстречу ему — тяжелые испарения буфета, едкая сигара, вокзальная гарь и косметика многотысячной толпы.

However, in the poem a particular concert is described. The iron world of the station is enchanted, and the music which the poet hears acquires a symbolic meaning.

Нельзя дышать, и твердь кишит червями,
И ни одна звезда не говорит,

Но, видит Бог, есть музыка над нами,
Дрожит вокзал от пенья аонид,
И снова, паровозными свистками
Разорванный, скрипичный воздух слит.

Огромный парк. Вокзала шар стеклянный.
Железный мир опять заворожен.
На звучный пир в элизиум туманный
Торжественно уносится вагон.
Павлиний крик и рокот фортепьянный —
Я опоздал. Мне страшно. Это сон.

И я вхожу в стеклянный лес вокзала,
Скрипичный строй в смятеньи и в слезах.
Ночного хора дикое начало,
И запах роз в гниющих парниках,
Где под стеклянным небом ночевала
Родная тень в кочующих толпах.

И мнится мне: весь в музыке и пене
Железный мир так нищенски дрожит,
В стеклянные я упираюсь сени;
Куда же ты? На тризне милой тени
В последний раз нам музыка звучит.[17]

Already the first impersonal sentence, "Nel'zja dyšat'", is significant for the general mood of the poem. The theme of air and breathing was very prominent in Mandel'štam's poetry in general. It is noteworthy that beginning in the early twenties the images of dense and unclear air and difficulty in breathing predominate. This theme is so complex that it should require a separate study. However, even a few quotations will be sufficient to illustrate its complexity:

Дыханье вещее в стихах моих
Животворящего их духа.

(1909?)

На стекла вечности уже легло
Мое дыхание, мое тепло.

(«Дано мне тело», 1909)

---

[17] In *Sobranie sočinenij* I (2nd ed.; 1967), the last stanza has the same number of lines (6) as the first three. The fourth line of the last stanza reads as follows: "Gorjačij par zrački smyčkov slepit". I am not convinced that Mandel'štam really intended to restore this line. Personally I prefer the five-line version. See also the note on pp. 462–463, where this addition is explained and where the reminiscences from Lermontov and Tjutčev are indicated.

К чему дышать? На жестких камнях пляшет
Больной удав, свиваясь и клубясь.
(«Осений сумрак», 1912)

Отравлен хлеб и *воздух выпит*,
Как трудно раны врачевать!
Иосиф, проданный в Египет,
Не мог сильнее тосковать!
(1913)

И сколько *воздуха* и шелка
И ветра в шёпоте твоем...
(«Твое чудесное произношенье», 1917)

Словно темную воду *я пью помутившийся воздух*...
(«Сестры — тяжесть и нежность», 1920)

Нельзя дышать, и твердь кишит червями...
(«Концерт на вокзале», 1921)

Приподнять, как *душный* стог,
Воздух, что шапкой томит...
(«Я не знаю, с каких пор», 1922)

Я дышал звезд млечной трухой,
Колтуном пространства *дышал*...
(«Я по лесенке приставной», 1922)

Воздух дрожит от сравнений...
— — — — — — — — —
Воздух бывает темным, как вода, и все живое в нем плавает как
рыба...
— — — — — — — — — — — —
Воздух замешан так же густо, как земля, —
Из него нельзя выйти, а в него трудно войти.
— — — — — — — — —
Хрупкое летоисчисление нашей эры подходит к концу.
(«Нашедший подкову», 1923)

Кремня и *воздуха* язык,
С прослойкой тьмы, с прослойкой света.
(«Грифельная ода», 1923)

Весь воздух выпила огромная гора...
(«Армения», VIII, 1930)

Кто-то чудной меня что-то торопит забыть, —
Душно, и все-таки до смерти хочется жить.
(«Колют ресницы», 1931)

Мне с каждым днем *дышать все тяжелее*,
А между тем нельзя повременить —

И рождены для наслажденья бегом
Лишь сердце человека и коня.

(«Сегодня можно...», 1931)

Люблю появление ткани,
Когда после двух или трех,
А то четырех *задыханий*
Придет выпрямительный вздох.

(«Восьмистишия», I—II, 1933)

Так, чтобы умереть на самом деле,
Тысячу раз на дню лишусь обычной
Свободы вздоха и сознанья цели.[18]

(Декабрь 1933)

А через *воздух сумрачно-хлопчатый*
Неначатой стены мерещатся зубцы ...

(«Бежит волна», 1935)

О, этот медленный, *одышливый простор* —
Я им пресыщен до отказа! —
И *отдышавшийся* распахнут кругозор —
Повязку бы на оба глаза.

(1937)

Я обращался *к воздуху слуге*,
Ждал от него услуги или вести
И собирался в путь, и плавал по дуге
Неначинающихся путешествий.

(«Не сравнивай», 1937)

Народу нужен свет и воздух голубой,
И нужен хлеб и снег Эльбруса.

(«Я нынче в паутине световой», 1937)

Я в яму, в бородавчатую темь,
Скольжу к обледенелой водокачке,
И, задыхаясь, мертвый воздух ем,
И разлетаются грачи в горячке.

(«Куда мне деться», 1937)

---

[18] In *Sobranie sočinenij* (Vol. I, 2nd ed.) these three lines are published as the second part of a six-line poem (No. 287, dated December, 1933). However, this is not an original poem by Mandel'štam, but a variant of lines 9–14 of his translation of the 164th sonnet by Petrarch, published in the same edition as No. 489 (dated December, 1933, — January, 1934). In the full text of the sonnet the end is different:

Тысячу раз на дню, себе на диво,
Я должен умереть на самом деле —
И воскресаю так же сверхобычно.

The later version is closer to the original.

Нам союзно лишь то что избыточно,
Впереди не провал, а промер,
И бороться за *воздух прожиточный* —
Это слава другим не в пример.

(«Стихи о неизвестном солдате», 1937)

А грудь стесняется, без языка тиха,
Уже не я пою — *поет мое дыханье*.
Песнь одноглазая, растущая из мха,
Одноголосый дар охотничьего быта,
Которую поют верхом и на верхах,
Держа дыханье вольно и открыто.

(«Пою, когда гортань сыра», 1937)

Что ж мне под голову другой песок подложен?
Ты — горловой Урал, плечистое Поволжье
Иль этот ровный край — вот все мои права, —
И полной грудью их *вдыхать еще я должен*.

(«Разрывы круглых бухт», 1937)

Если б меня лишили всего в мире —
Права дышать и открывать двери
И утверждать, что бытие будет . . .
— — — — — — — — — — — — — — —
Я не смолчу . . .

(«Если б меня наши враги взяли», 1937)

And finally, only one quotation from Mandel'štam's prose:

Все произведения мировой литературы я делю на разрешенные и написанные без разрешения. Первые — это мразь, вторые — *ворованный воздух*.

(«Четвертая проза», 1930—1931)

I believe that these quotations speak for themselves.

The image of the unfriendly sky was familiar to Mandel'štam's early poetry.

. . . неживого небосвода
Всегда смеющийся хрусталь!

(«Сусальным золотом горят», 1908)

Я вижу каменное небо
Над тусклой паутиной вод.
— — — — — — — —
Я понимаю этот ужас
И постигаю эту связь:
И небо падает, не рушась,
И море плещет, не пенясь.

(1909?)

Я вижу месяц бездыханный
И небо мертвенней холста...
                        («Слух чуткий парус напрягает»,1910)

Твердь умолкла, умерла...
                        («Скудный луч холодной мерою», 1911)

Небо тусклое с отсветом странным —
Мировая туманная боль...
                        («Воздух пасмурный влажен и гулок», 1911)

О небо, небо, ты мне будешь сниться!
Не может быть, чтоб ты совсем ослепло...
                                                    (1911)

But never had his sky been as hostile and frightening as it was in "Koncert na vokzale".

In the first line of this poem, the image of the sky[19] swarming

---

[19] There is no doubt in my mind that the word *tverd* in "Koncert na vokzale" means 'sky', 'firmament'. The entire image of the first stanza is ascensional, as it were: first the suffocating atmosphere ("nel'zja dyšat'"), then the blackness of the sky swarming with worms, then the stars, and finally — the music which is *above us*.

In Russian poetic usage, the word *tverd* primarily refers to the sky. When it means 'earth', 'terra firma', it is usually used in combination with sky ("nebo i tverd") or it is modified by the adjective *zemnaja*. Mandel'štam used this noun seven times in his poetry, but never in the sense of 'earth'.

In five instances it means the actual sky:

(1)   *Твердь* умолкла, умерла.
      С колокольни отуманенной
      Кто-то снял колокола.
                        («Скудный луч холодной мерою», 1911)

(2)   Только там, где *твердь светла*,
      Черно-желтый лоскут злится.
                        («Дворцовая площадь», 1917)

(3)   Нельзя дышать и *твердь кишит червями*...
                        («Концерт на вокзале», 1921)

(4)   Умывался ночью на дворе —
      Твердь сияла грубыми звездами...
                                                    (1921)

(5)   Под высокую руку берет
      Побежденную *твердь* Азраил.
                        («Ветер нам утешенье принес», 1922)

There is a striking similarity between examples (3) and (4). Both were written in the same year, and in both an unfriendly sky is depicted.

with worms may have been suggested by David Burljuk's poem "Mertvoe nebo" (published in the almanac *Doxlaja luna*, 1913):

«Небо труп! не больше!
Звезды — *черви* — пьяные туманом
Усмиряю боль ше-лестом обманом
Небо — смрадный труп!!²⁰

One could dislike this poem, and I would not blame anybody for it. One may well recall the lines by Axmatova:

Когда б вы знали, из какого сора
Растут стихи, не ведая стыда!

If Mandel'štam actually took the image of worms from Burljuk, this fact may be interesting, on the one hand, because it contributes to our understanding of his creative process and, on the other hand, as an evidence of his exquisite memory, but such a subtext does not afford a deeper comprehension of his poem.

The second line of the poem contains an overt poetic polemic with Lermontov's lines:

Ночь тиха. Пустыня внемлет Богу,
И звезда с звездою говорит.
В небесах торжественно и чудно...

In Mandel'štam, a strong sensation of an impending cataclysm is sharply opposed to Lermontov's sense of cosmic harmony.

Mandel'štam will return to the image of Lermontovian cosmos in "Grifel'naja oda" (1923):

To the best of my understanding, in the remaining two instances *tverd'* also means 'sky': the sky painted on a porcelain plate (*stekljannaja tverd'* in "Na blednoguluboj èmali", 1909), or on the wall (*stenobitnaja tverd'* in "Tajnaja večerja", 1937).

[20] There is a difference, however, between Mandel'štam's and Burljuk's sky. In Mandel'štam, the black visible firmament is full of worms; in Burljuk the worms are the stars themselves.

An inquisitive reader may ask whether Burljuk's poem does not already contain a hidden polemic with Lermontov's "Vyxožu odin ja na dorogu", Is it not the Lermontovian mist in the second line of "Mertvoe nebo" (which, incidentally, is a trochaic pentameter)? Even if Burljuk did not have Lermontov in mind, could not Mandel'štam understand his poem as a polemic with Lermontov and drive the point home?

See my article "Tri zametki o poèzii Mandel'štama", *IJSLP* XII (1969), 165-166.

Звезда с звездой могучий стык,
Кремнистый путь из старой песни...

and in "Stixi o neizvestnom soldate" (1937):

Научи меня, ласточка хилая,
Разучившаяся летать,
Как мне с этой *воздушной могилою*
Без руля и крыла совладать.

И за Лермонтова Михаила
Я отдам тебе строгий отчет,
Как сутулого учит могила
И *воздушная яма* влечет.

This is again a polemic with Lermontov. *Vozdušnaja jama*, with an obviously negative shade of meaning, is opposed to Lermontov's *vozdušnyj okean*:

На воздушном океане
Без руля и без ветрил
Тихо плавают в тумане
Хоры стройные светил.

Lermontov's voice is heard in "Koncert na vokzale" once more, in the last stanza. Mandel'štam's lines:

И мнится мне: весь в музыке и пене
Железный мир так нищенски дрожит...

may be compared with those by Lermontov:

И снился мне сияющий огнями
Вечерний пир в родимой стороне...

This is a clear case of borrowing *po ritmu i zvučaniju* (in Sergej Bobrov's terms).[21] Nevertheless, we may ask the question: why did this borrowing occur? The probable answer is that the theme of death (and dreaming of death: "Mne strašno. Èto son") is present both in the prophetic "Son" and in the apocalyptic "Koncert na vokzale".

There is, indeed, an apocalyptic mood in the image of a sky that swarms with worms, where all the stars are silent. There is also an apocalyptic purport in the pointed conclusion of the poem:

Куда же ты? На тризне милой тени
В последний раз нам музыка звучит.

---

[21] S. Bobrov, "Zaimstvovanija i vlijanija", *Pečať i revoljucija* VIII (1922), 72-92.

This conclusion echoes the fifth and the sixth line of the following poem by Tjutčev:

> Я лютеран люблю богослуженье,
> Обряд их строгий, важный и простой —
> Сих голых стен, сей храмины пустой
> Понятно мне высокое ученье.
>
> *Не видите ль? Собравшися в дорогу,*
> *В последний раз вам вера предстоит:*[22]
> Еще она не перешла порогу,
> Но дом ее уж пуст и гол стоит, —
>
> Еще она не перешла порогу,
> Еще за ней не затворилась дверь...
> Но час настал, пробил... Молитесь Богу,
> *В последний раз вы молитесь теперь.*

The mood here is apocalyptic, just as it is in Mandel'štam's poem.[23] Against the background of this subtext, the music in "Koncert na vokzale" acquires a higher meaning: it becomes a kind of religious rite.

The theme of death and music appears in Mandel'štam's poetry as early as 1912 in the poem "Pešexod". Here, as in "Koncert na vokzale", the poet is frightened by "mysterious heights", listening to the sound of a snow-ball which is on its way to becoming an avalanche, and will destroy him (and probably not only him). He is aware that music cannot rescue him from the abyss, despite the fact that his whole soul is "in the bells":

> Действительно, лавина есть в горах!
> И вся моя душа — в колоколах,
> Но музыка от бездны не спасет!

The last line of the poem may suggest a polemic with Skrjabin's belief that the power of music can save humanity.[24]

---

[22] Mandel'štam's conclusion of "Koncert na vokzale" repeats even the rhythmo-syntactic pattern of these lines (and *zvučit* rhymes with *predstoit*).

[23] One may further compare Tjutčev's "golye steny" and "pustaja xramina" with Mandel'štam's "vokzala šar stekljannyj", "železnyj mir", and "stekljannyj les vokzala": the concert, like the Lutheran service, is held in austere surroundings.

[24] "... dlja Skrjabina xarakterno to, čto Iskupitelem, kotoryj prineset s soboj novoe nebo i novuju zemlju, budet muzykant, artist, a ne moraľnyj propovednik, pričem imenno xudožnik prineset miru vseobščuju garmoniju — ljubov' i spravedlivosť"(I. I. Lapšin, *Zavetnye dumy Skrjabina* [Petrograd 1922], 23).

There is one puzzling image in the last stanza of "Koncert na vokzale": *trizna miloj teni*, which should be explained. One can guess that the poet is mourning a Russia which is gone forever, and primarily her cultural past. The reader who recalls another of Tjutčev's poems, "Duša moja — Èlizium tenej", will be assured that his guess is correct. It should be recalled that the image of Elysium appears both in Mandel'štam's prosaic description of the concert and in the poem.

> Душа моя — Элизиум теней,
> Теней безмолвных, светлых и прекрасных,
> Ни помыслам годины буйной сей,
> Ни радостям, ни горю не причастных.
> Душа моя, Элизиум теней,
> Что общего меж жизнью и тобою!
> Меж вами, *призраки минувших, лучших дней*,
> И сей бесчувственной толпою?..

I believe that the first subtext by Lermontov and both subtexts by Tjutčev contribute to a better understanding of the very message of Mandel'štam's poem.[25] They are important, and their function is entirely different from that of Burljuk's subtext, which may be ignored.

A remarkable note has been found among Mandel'štam's papers. It deals with the idea of reading one poet and hearing the voice of another.

2 мая 31 г. Чтенье Некрасова. «Влас» и «Жил на свете рыцарь бедный».

Некрасов

> Говорят, ему видение
> Все мерещилось в бреду:
> Видел света преставление,
> Видел грешников в аду.

---

[25] There may be third subtext by Tjutčev in "Koncert na vokzale", the image of the dear shadow *(milaja ten')* possibly coming from the last stanza of Tjutčev's poem "Ona sidela na polu":

> Стоял я молча в стороне
> И пасть готов был на колени, —
> И страшно грустно стало мне,
> *Как от присущей милой тени.*

Пушкин

> Он имел одно виденье,
> Недоступное уму,
> И глубоко впечатленье
> В сердце врезалось ему.

«С той поры» — и дальше как бы слышится второй потаенный голос:

> Lumen coelum, Sancta Rosa...

Та же фигура стихотворная, та же тема отозвания и подвига.

If we define the context as a set of texts which contain the same or a similar image, the subtext may be defined as an already existing text (or texts) reflected in a new one.

There are four kinds of subtexts: (1) that which serves as a simple impulse for the creation of an image; (2) *zaimstvovanie po ritmu i zvučaniju* (borrowing of a rhythmic figure and the sounds contained therein); (3) the text which supports or reveals the poetic message of a later text; (4) the text which is treated polemically by the poet. The first two do not necessarily contribute to our better understanding of a given poem. However, (2) may be combined with (3) and/or (4), and (3) and (4) may, in their turn, be blended.

It is self-evident that the concept of context and subtext may overlap in cases of self-quotations and autoreminiscences. This happens often in Mandel'štam's poetry. For example, in the poem "Čto pojut časy-kuznečik" (1917) there is an image of a sinking boat:

> ...зубами мыши точат
> Жизни тоненькое дно...
> ...ласточка и дочка[26]
> Отвязала мой челнок...
> Но черемуха услышит
> *И на дне морском: прости.*
> ...смерть невинна...

This bidding farewell to life and its simple beauty[27] is repeated in the poem "Telefon" (1918):

---

[26] I.e., lastočka–dočka.

[27] In Russian minds, the unpretentious, fragrant bloom of *čeremuxa* (the so-called "European bird-cherry" is associated with the beauty and poetry of everyday life. Cf. my article "Razbor odnogo 'zaumnogo' stixotvorenija Mandel'štama", *Russian Literature* 2 (1972), 132–151; about the image of *čeremuxa* see particularly pp. 147–149.

В высоком строгом кабинете
Самоубийцы — телефон...
Звонок — и закружились сферы:
Самоубийство решено...
Молчи, проклятая шкатулка!
На дне морском цветет: прости!

For a person who does not know the first poem the image may be surprising, even enigmatic.

Harvard University